# Your Black & White

# Family Wild

# Arts

# Manual

## Kim Nunneley

## M.W. Nunneley

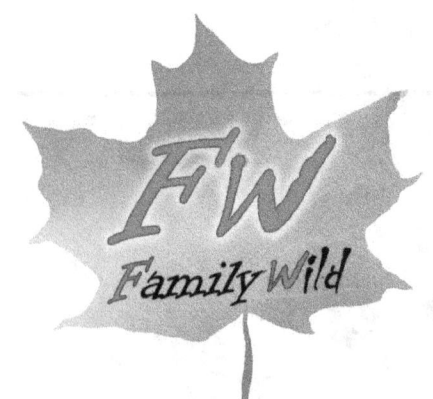

# Family Wild

# Club

# Registration

Register Your Club for free at:

**www.familywildprogram.com**

on the Contact Page

## Give your club a name like <u>Nunneley Family Wild</u> and register it to join the Family Wild Nation!

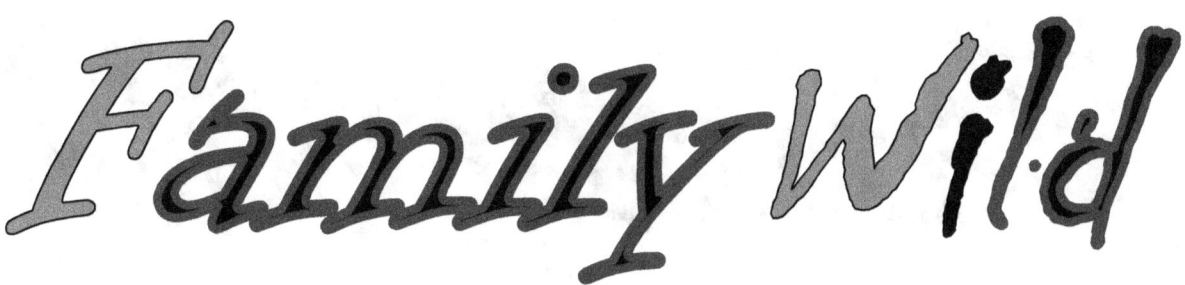

# Family Wild

"CREATIVITY is allowing
yourself to make mistakes.
Art is knowing which ones
to keep."

Author Unknown

# Family Wild

"Every child is an artist. The problem is how to remain an artist once he grows up."

Pablo Picasso

# Family Wild Library

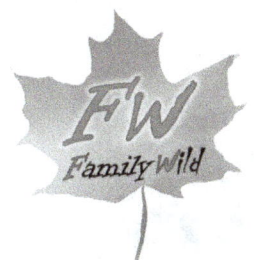
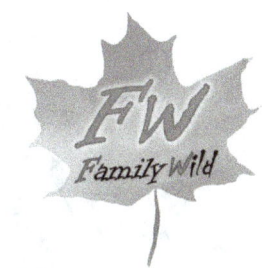

Your Family Wild Hunting Club Manual
Your Family Wild Fishing Club Manual
Your Family Wild Arts Club Manual

Your Family Wild Hunting SLAM Journal
Your Family Wild Fishing SLAM Journal
Your Family Wild Arts SLAM Journal

Your Family Wild Hunting Activities Handbook - Volume I
Your Family Wild Fishing Activities Handbook - Volume I
Your Family Wild Arts Activities Handbook - Volume I

Your Family Wild Annual Hunting Record Book
Your Family Wild Annual Fishing Record Book
Your Family Wild ALL-TIME Hunting Record Book
Your Family Wild ALL-TIME Fishing Record Book

## Full Color vs Black & White???

*Family Wild understands that families face financial challenges every day. As a result, we release a Full Color Version of our books as well as a more affordable Black & White text. We want you to enjoy our Family Wild publications without breaking your bank. The information contained in the Color version and the Black & White titles are EXACTLY the same. By publishing both, as with everything Family Wild, we let you decide what works best for YOU! Enjoy!*
*- M.W. Nunneley*

## Coming Soon!

Your Family Wild Hunting Beginner's Coloring Book
Your Family Wild Fishing Advanced Coloring Book

Your Family Wild Photography Book

Your Family Wild Deer Blind Diaries
Your Family Wild Deer Camp Diaries
Your Family Wild Fish Tales
Your Family Wild Hunting Camp Journal
Your Family Wild Fishing Journal
Your Family Wild White-Tail Deer Harvest Journal

Your Family Wild Hunting Camp Cookbook
Your Family Wild Fishing Recipe Book
Your Family Wild Trail Camera Log

# Family Wild

"*I presume, sir, in painting your beautiful portrait (of me), you took your idea of me from my principles, and not from my person.*"

Abraham Lincoln

**Family Wild, LLC**
**Email address: familywild@familywildprogram.com**

**Website: www.familywildprogram.com**

**Family Wild Online Store - www.familywildprogram.com**

**Facebook - https://www.facebook.com/Familywild2016/**

The information provided within this Book is for general informational purposes only. While we try to keep the information up-to-date and correct, there are no representations or warranties, express or implied, about the completeness, accuracy, reliability, suitability or availability with respect to the information, products, services, or related graphics contained in this Book for any purpose. Any use of this information is at your own risk and the risk of your friends and family.

The information contained within this Book is strictly for educational purposes. If you wish to apply ideas contained in this Book, you are taking full responsibility for your actions.

ISBN-13: 978-1546966203

ISBN-10: 154696620X

Cover Illustration Copyright © 2017 M.W. Nunneley
Cover design by M.W. Nunneley
Editing by Kim Nunneley
Author photograph by Del Beyer

# Family Wild

"Every artist dips his brush in his own soul,
and paints his own nature into his pictures."

Henry Ward Beecher
19th Century American Clergyman

# *Family Wild*

## For Courtney & Ian -

Like family before us,

pass on your love of the arts,

hunting & fishing

to your own children, grandchildren,

nieces & nephews.

# *Family Wild*

"Never Grow Up. Adults don't have any fun!"

Teacher - Ann Tabor

# Family Wild

## Acknowledgements

**To all the children in my life (some of them in their 80's) who reminded me to play, to unconsciously create and dance and laugh and to be awed by our natural world.**

**This book is for you.**

**- Kim**

# Family Wild

"If you're going to break a law of art, make the crime interesting."

Mason Cooley
*American Aphorist*

# Your Black & White Family Wild Art Club Manual
# Table of Contents

# *Family Wild*

"There are no great limits to growth because there are no limits of human intelligence, imagination, and wonder."

President Ronald Reagan

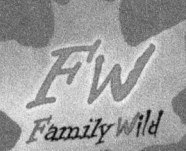

# Family Wild

## Chapter
## 1
## Welcome

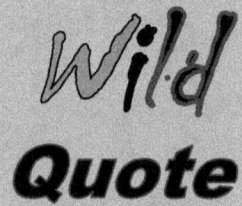

# Wild Quote

*"Art is the*

*only way to*

*run away*

*without*

*leaving*

*home."*

**Author
Unknown**

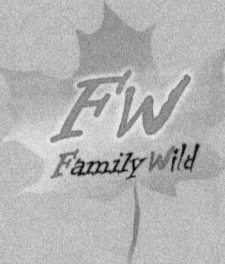

# Family Wild Motto

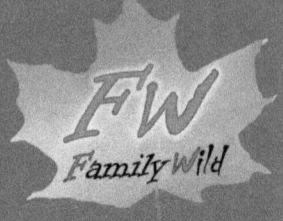

*"Hunting, Fishing, Loving Every Day!"*

**Luke Bryan**
Country Singer

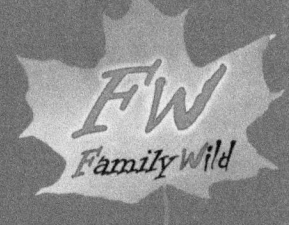

# Welcome

## *Objective - Get Family Wild*

*Family Wild* sprang to life in 2016 as a way to connect family members to each other through the nature sports of hunting and fishing, as well as the arts that call us to interact with all things wild. This book shows you how to create your own *Family Wild* club.

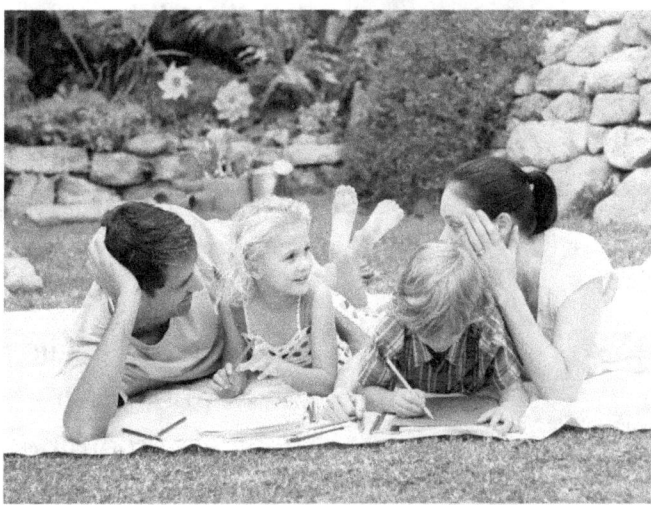

Creating your own **Family Wild** Club encourages YOUR family and friends - children, teens, parents, grandparents – the entire unit of family and friends - to gather regularly to create and celebrate the natural environment through activities, images, words, delicious food, and the construction of practical outdoor, fishing and hunting aids.

**Family Wild** emphasizes families and friends **DOING THINGS TOGETHER IN NATURE.** The more you take this to heart, the richer your *Family Wild* experience.

We encourage children, teens and adults to log their accomplishments and strive to earn "Slam" achievement certificates.

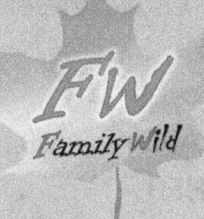

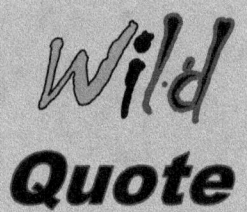

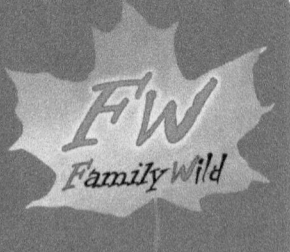

# Welcome

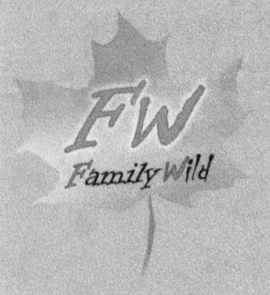

We've filled the **Family Wild** library of books with great activities and projects for your entire family.

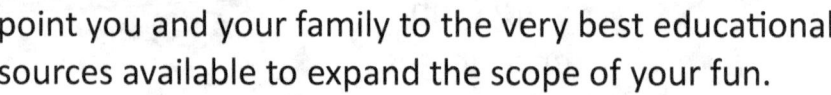

Further, we offer you FREE additional programing at the **Family Wild** website and blog. This allows us to point you and your family to the very best educational sources available to expand the scope of your fun.

We've tried to keep our activities relatively low cost and family friendly. Allow your children to do as much as they can on their own - don't let your own expectations limit their resourcefulness. Given the opportunity, your children will stun you with what they can actually accomplish when they set their minds to it.

*"I recall watching my son, an avowed computer geek, build his first 2x4 wall and clean his first squirrel - only then did I realize his abilities far exceeded my expectations."*

*- Kim Nunneley*

When you do need to step in and help, remember to keep a sense of humor and play. Dare to **CREATE** precious and fun-filled **Family Wild** memories **TOGETHER.**

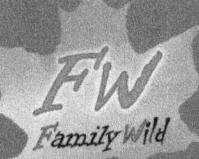

# Family Wild

## Chapter
## 2
## Getting Started

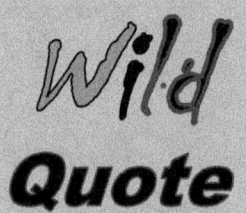

# Getting Started

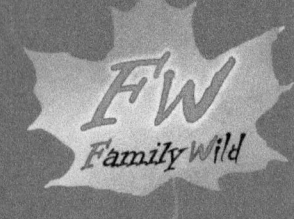

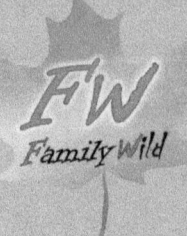

## Creating your Family Wild Chapter

YOU decide how easy or detailed, small or large, you want to make your chapter of *Family Wild*. YOU OWN YOUR CLUB. However, we encourage you to follow the process of a typical club or organization for several reasons.

First, it makes it REAL for all, especially your younger members. If they played basketball or joined a Scout Troup or any other club they would have some kind of Articles of Incorporation, by-laws, officers, duties and expectations.

We suggest you make this feel as real as any other group. The more "official" you make it, the more respect you'll create from all your members and the more your kids will learn.

Second, official groups have regular meetings - the **_MOST IMPORTANT_** reason to set up your Chapter in such an "official" manner. As people of all ages find themselves busier than ever, setting regular meetings will keep *Family Wild* top-of-mind.

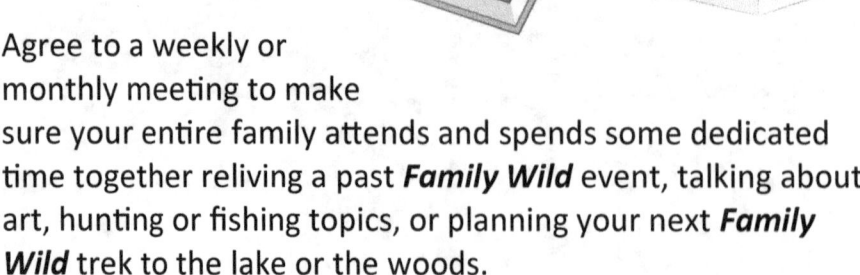

Agree to a weekly or monthly meeting to make sure your entire family attends and spends some dedicated time together reliving a past *Family Wild* event, talking about art, hunting or fishing topics, or planning your next *Family Wild* trek to the lake or the woods.

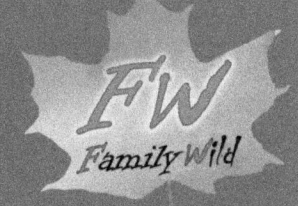
"Art enables us to find ourselves and lose our selves at the same time."

**Thomas Merton** Trappist Monk

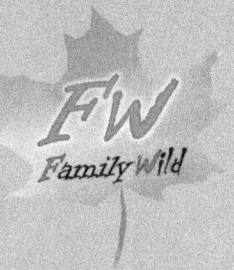

Third, we strongly encourage you elect your younger members to positions of responsibility. Depending on their age, you may have to assist them in completing their duties and responsibilities, but this allows them to take pride in a leadership position and teaches them the "pressures" of such roles.

**CAUTION:** *Let patience guide you* - let your kids come up with their own ideas, help nurture them, and even let them mess something up or "fail." Sometimes you need to let them fly as high as they can - and have a pillow ready when they fall.

Parents, don't forget to let your children grow, but keep the fun and excitement for your family alive. We've all had a boss, teacher, coach (or even a parent) who took the fun out of an activity.

Trust us - the more you encourage your children to come up with their own ideas, do their own work, create their own excitement, the more individual growth you'll see from your children.

Fourth, we recommend you have a finance committee and dues. Make the dues affordable, but having "skin" in the deal makes it real. Many hunting camps have dues and most sport teams charge some type of fee. Make this real life and charge for membership - of course you all get to keep this fee and use it towards your *Family Wild* events.

We even suggest you make them pay for it themselves or "earn" the money doing family work (i.e. snow blowing, cleaning the dishes, cutting grass). It won't hurt them a bit and will teach them the value of their *Family Wild* membership and money.

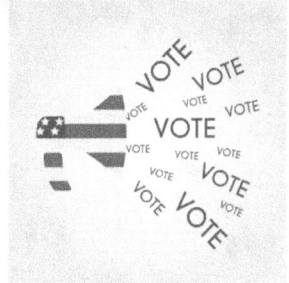

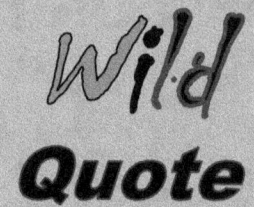

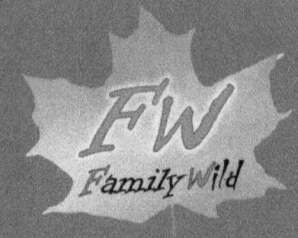

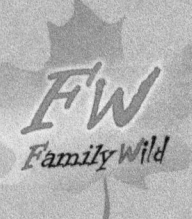

# Family Wild

## Create your Family Wild Chapter

I. Conduct First Chapter Meeting

II. Review and Approve By-Laws

III. Elect Officers

IV. Establish Committees

V. Create Regular Meeting Times

VI. Discuss and Decide Your First Family Wild Event

VII. New Business

IX. Open Discussion

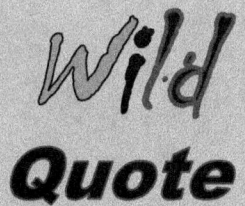

# Wild Quote

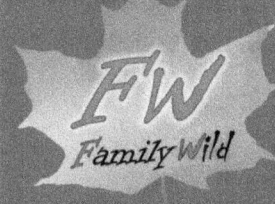

# Club Contact List

*"It is easier to go down a hill than up it but the view is much better at the top."*

**Henry Ward Beecher** 19th Century Clergyman

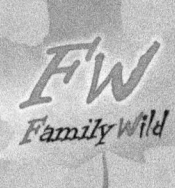

| # | Name | Address | Phone Number | Email |
|---|------|---------|--------------|-------|
| 1 | | | | |
| 2 | | | | |
| 3 | | | | |
| 4 | | | | |
| 5 | | | | |
| 6 | | | | |
| 7 | | | | |
| 8 | | | | |
| 9 | | | | |
| 10 | | | | |
| 11 | | | | |
| 12 | | | | |
| 13 | | | | |
| 14 | | | | |
| 15 | | | | |

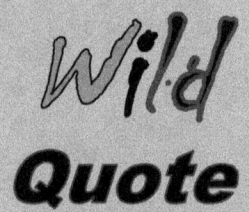

# Wild Quote

"Art washes away the dust of everyday life."

**Pablo Picasso**
Spanish Artist

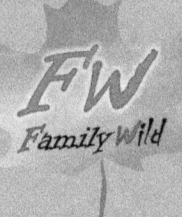

# Typical Agenda

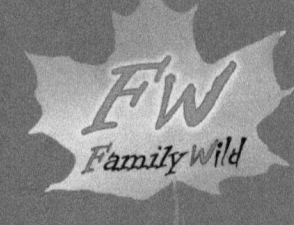

## Family Wild

I. Call to Order

II. Treasurer's Report

III. Committee Reports

IV. Guest Speaker - if scheduled

V. Pre/Post Event Report

VI. Pre/Post Tournament Report

VII. Old Business

VIII. New Business

IX. Open Discussion

X. Close Meeting

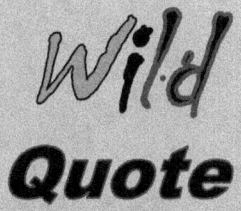

# Officers

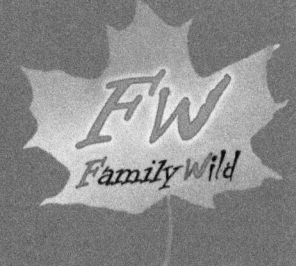

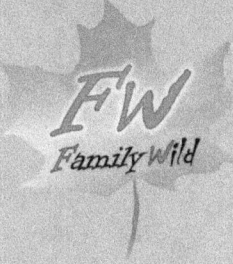
# Electing Officers

When creating your **Family Wild** club, we suggest you elect officers. We recommend the following offices for **Family Wild**:

- **President**
- **Vice President**
- **Secretary**
- **Treasurer**
- **Public Relations**

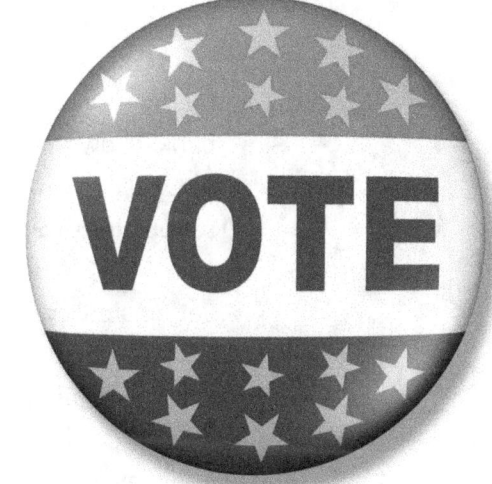

You can make their duties as simple or as detailed as you wish. If you look in the back of the book, you'll see an example of by-laws and the duties of officers.

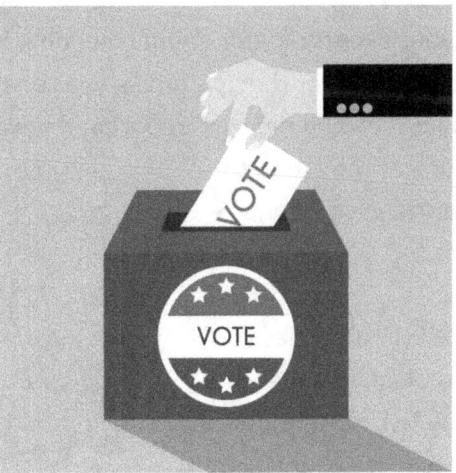

You may require an adult serve as President but maybe an older child as Vice President and Treasurer of your club. Take this opportunity to give your children responsibility and help them with their tasks. To this day, I use the skills I learned from clubs I joined and leadership positions I held as a child and teen.

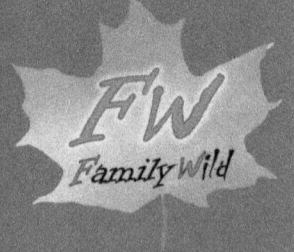

## *Family Wild* Finances

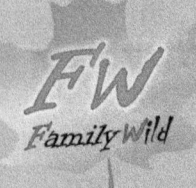
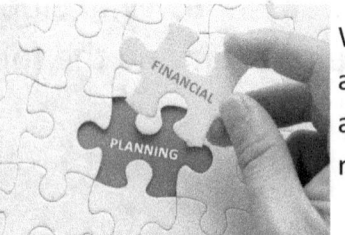

We suggest electing one of your older children as the Treasurer, typically Junior or Senior High age. You can also include other younger members on your Finance Committee.

Go with the treasurer and other finance members and open a free checking and savings account at a credit union or bank. Show them how to record the money coming in and the money going out. Help them understand how to write a check, use online banking, and set up alerts to protect the accounts.

Set up a policy that 10 or 20% of dues go into the Chapter's savings account for emergencies. Order a debit card that an adult holds and can use for small purchases of items for events.

You may want to brainstorm fundraisers for your *Family Wild* Club to generate extra money for your club's activities. You might wash cars or pick and sell strawberries, or charge a nominal fee for tournaments to finance your next activity. You're only limited by your collective imagination and commitment.

When you have your events or your annual meeting, help your young Treasurer create a budget for the up-coming year or activity. Assist them in creating the annual year-end financial report and have them present it at the regular meeting of the group to illustrate the importance of money matters.

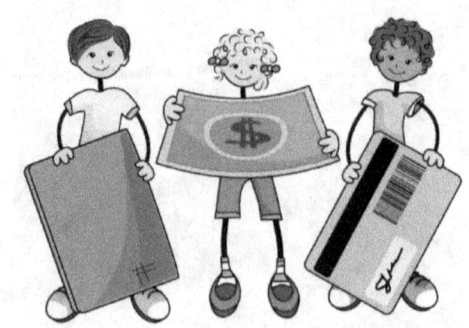

Trust us, of all the FUN activities you'll enjoy with *Family Wild*, you may find handling money is THE most important skill *Family Wild* teaches your children or grandchildren.

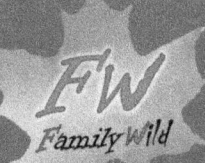
# Family Wild

## Chapter

## 3

## Member Activity

## Submissions

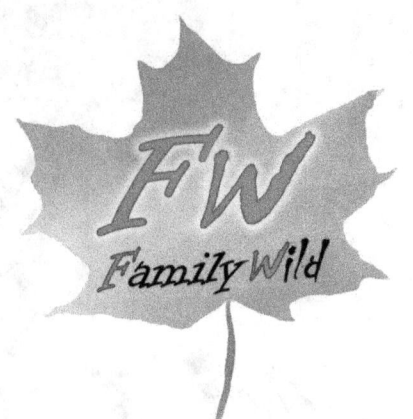

# Family Wild Activities

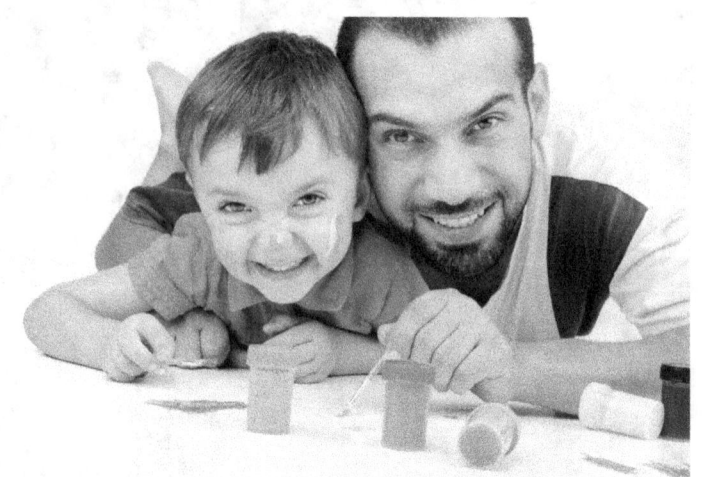

Throughout this section, we'll give you a taste of our *Family Wild* **Activities Books.** Our activities collection is a continuing series of publications offering you a variety of projects and group fun for your *Family Wild* club.

While tournaments may occur monthly or one weekend during a particular hunting or fishing season, you can enjoy activities after work, during school vacations, or even on weekends.

## IMPORTANT ANNOUNCEMENT

## FAMILY WILD needs <u>YOUR</u> help.

Although we have a bunch of great ideas for activities, we know we don't have them all. So, we want you to submit your ideas and pictures of you doing your activities to us at *Family Wild*.

We want art, hunting or fishing activities, no matter how big or small, simple or complicated. We also want ideas for fishing and hunting themes that incorporate writing, painting, photography, sculpture, videography, gardening, recipes and cooking or construction like blinds and bird feeders.

*Family Wild* will then go through the submissions to pick the very best ideas for our next release. If we select yours, we'll send you a complimentary edition!

Look for additional information later in this book or visit our website at **www.familywildprogram.com** for details about how to make your activity and family famous in future *Family Wild* publications.

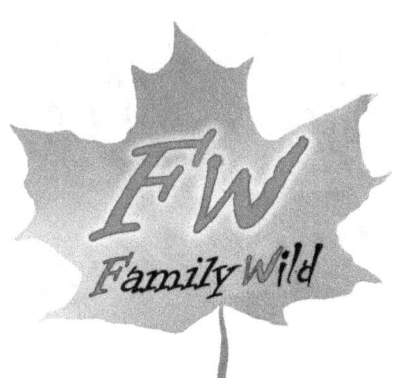

# Family Wild Activities

At **Family Wild**, we love hearing the story behind your activity. As a result, we ask that you give us the fun details of the activity. You also may want to give your activity to someone outside of your family to review or try to make sure you've made it "doable" for someone unfamiliar with your type of hunting, fishing or art. Keep in mind, we target both world class folks as well as young beginners with our activities.

### Ask yourself the following questions when you summarize your activity:

*Who can do this activity? Is there an age group that should do this or, more importantly, shouldn't? Should parts of this project be done by an adult?*

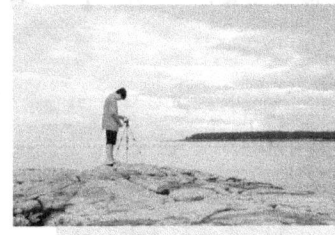

*What is the activity? What supplies do you need? What tools? What part of the activity is more child-friendly? What challenges may arise? What safety concerns should you consider?*

*How long will this activity take? Can you accomplish this in minutes, hours, or do you need a weekend or longer?*

*Where should this activity occur? Should part of it be done at home or camp and the other in the field or on the lake?*

*Why would you want to try this activity? What are your goals for everyone who attempts this?*

*How do you go about preparing for this activity? How do you begin?*

*Finally, and in our opinion, most important, tell us the "family story" behind your activity. Who taught you or who have you taught? Tell us the history: the good, the bad, the ugly and the funny.*

Please include pictures of your family doing the activity. Remember, you'll need to complete our Photo Releases for all adults and children (found in the Appendix or our website **www.familywildprogram.com.**) Also fill out the Activity Cover Sheet as well as the Intellectual Property Release.

With a little luck, we'll publish YOUR FAMILY'S experience in our next activity book and, if we do, we'll send you a free copy as our thank you.

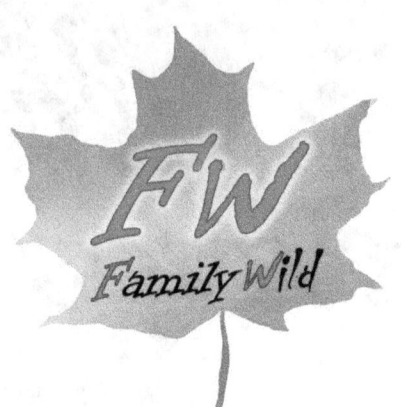

The **Family Wild** Activity Series of Books came from night crawler picking of all things. My Grandmother (yes, Grandmother) taught all of her grandchildren how to pick crawlers and worms at night after a summer rain.

Imagine a four-foot, eleven-inch tall Night Crawler Ninja stalking like a preying mantis, flashlight in one hand and fingers near the ground with the other, waiting to cobra strike the unsuspecting fish bait.

All the grandchildren learned that Grandma and Grandpa had a small gas station and bait shop on Long Lake. They picked crawlers to sell to put money in the till and food on the table. At sixty years old, Grandma ended up teaching a gaggle of grandkids the all-but-lost art of hunting their own fishing bait as well as a family tradition we all still laugh about when we remember Grandma.

Flash forward 40 years. I took my new wife, Kim, and step-son, Ian, crawler picking. As we jumped out of the car with flashlights in hand, they both proceeded to stomp through the yard like two Transformers headed to battle. "STOP!" I begged. They both looked at me puzzled and confused.

As I worked my way in front of them, I immediately went into our family's traditional Night Crawler Ninja position. As I crept forward, light shining the ground for the little crawlers, I heard giggles behind me. My loving wife and step-son couldn't contain themselves at the presence of the six-foot tall, 299.5 pound, Night Crawler Ninja.

Now I must admit, given my sense of humor, I understood how they may have concluded they had boarded another Michael practical joke bus, fully equipped with lights and buckets, in search of giant night crawlers. They both sounded as if they knew the punch line to the joke and couldn't contain themselves, until...

...the FLASH of the Night Crawler Ninja's right hand plucked an unsuspecting giant worm from its hole in the ground. Suddenly silence replaced giggles as they watched the struggle between hunter and hunted. Success!!!

A few minutes later, Kim and Ian joined generations of my family as they prowled the back yard for the next day's fishing bait. Although neither met the Ninja Sensei, they both learned a craft that started for me and my family with Grandma Marie, the original Night Crawler Ninja Warrior.

Thus began what would become the **Family Wild** Activities model. In our activity books, we want to share the stories of outdoor activities you've learned from your grandparents, parents, family or friends. More importantly, we want to encourage you to pass these traditions on to your children/grandchildren and allow **Family Wild** to share them with other members.

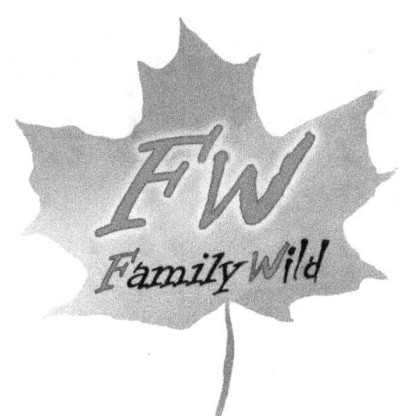

Hunters, fisherman and artist all come with a bag of tricks they guarantee will help you bag a bigger buck, grab your limit or create something astonishing. If you want to watch an old outdoorsman's or artist eyes beam, ask them how they hunt for this, fish for that, or create their craft and then grab a chair and get comfortable.

Sometimes, you just learn things in the moment. For example, my Grandfather Ken told me you always troll walleyes with 100 feet of line and a Rapala lure behind the pontoon. I still clean rabbits the way my Grandpa Cranston showed me how to do as a teenager. To this day, I still compare every jar of homemade strawberry jelly to my Grandma Gertrude's. Oh, I forgot to mention, the Night Crawler Ninja, Grandma Marie, also showed me the patience of unscrambling the fishing line tangle, otherwise known as a "nest-mess."

Please don't think we won't find your activity interesting or worthy of publishing. In most cases, we may find the story behind the activity actually determines what we publish.

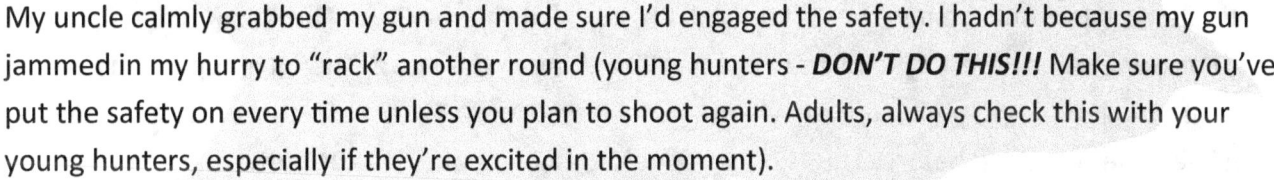

Let me give you an example. After I shot my first buck as a 16 year-old, I ran (picture the Stay Puff Marshmallow Man in hunter orange) to camp to get my Uncle Gary to help me track my deer. As I entered the camp huffing and puffing, I stammered that I'd shot a buck.

My uncle calmly grabbed my gun and made sure I'd engaged the safety. I hadn't because my gun jammed in my hurry to "rack" another round (young hunters - ***DON'T DO THIS!!!*** Make sure you've put the safety on every time unless you plan to shoot again. Adults, always check this with your young hunters, especially if they're excited in the moment).

Then my Uncle Gary told me to do the darndest thing I'd ever heard. He told me to get a roll of toilet paper. Dumbfounded, I literally replied "I didn't mess my pants and I don't need to go to the bathroom." He laughed and told me we would use the sheets of toilet paper to mark the blood stains on the leaf covered autumn ground. The white toilet paper would allow us to relocate the blood trail, should we lose it.

This is just one example of a wisdom - nugget I've never forgotten and will pass on to the next generation of Nunneley *Family Wild* hunters.

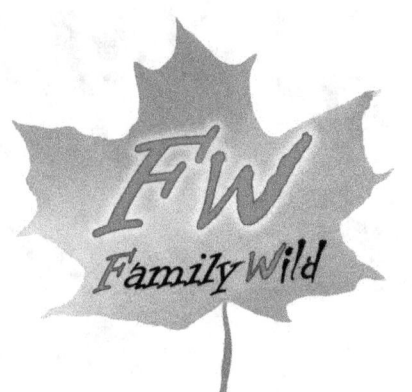

# Family Wild Activities

At **Family Wild**, we've tried to include options and activities for everyone. Maybe your spouse doesn't enjoy hunting or fishing. Maybe your middle child lives for the woods but doesn't care for fishing. On the other hand, your oldest loves photography or videography but doesn't like to hunt. Bringing up the rear, your youngest loves to go to camp and loves to sit in the blind but hates anything icky.

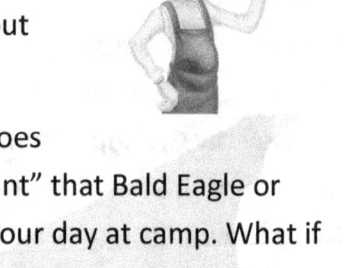

As a result, we want to offer activities for everyone. Maybe your family goes for long rides looking for wildlife and you keep a camera in the car to "hunt" that Bald Eagle or Snowy Owl. Perhaps your youngest always writes in their journal about your day at camp. What if your spouse paints a bird scene? All of these activities could find their way into our next activity book. Just make sure to highlight your **Family Wild** STORY along with the activity.

Looking for another great opportunity for you to pass on your tradition? Send us your FAMOUS wildlife-based recipes. Of course, we want mouth-watering meals from the field *and* the store. You don't have to kill it to submit a favorite dish for the **Family Wild** Recipes Book.

For example, at our camp, Coach always whipped up a venison meal that left everyone 10 pounds heavier and EVERY DISH DIRTIED IN THE CAMP. The "kids" didn't want dish detail when Coach took over the kitchen. The fun of this camp story was the mountain of dirty dishes that appeared year after year.

Another example would be my "world famous" Chili. I call it the my Clean Out The Kitchen Chili. First, I buy one can of every type of bean or bean-like thing in the store. Then, I go up and down the aisle searching for anything that may work in my concoction. Every year, there has to be one thing I've never included before. This is how Nestle's Chocolate and peanut butter have both found their ways into my creation. I always put in 2 pounds of ground venison. Finally, the determining factor to see if it's done? I check to see if a soup ladle stands straight up in the middle of it. Every family has that story that surrounds a special meal. Put yours into 400-500 words along with the recipe and see if makes our upcoming **Family Wild** *Recipe Guide*. Again, if your entry makes the book, we'll send you a free copy as our thank you. Submit to

## *FamilyWild@familywildprogram.com*

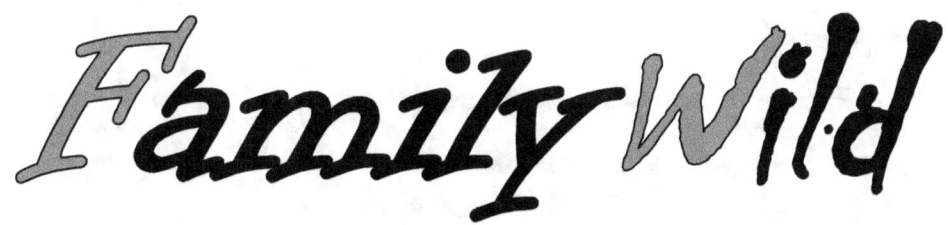

# Family Wild Activity

## Application Form

Applicant Name _____

Address _____

Phone # _____

Email Address _____

Activity Name _____

## Items Included with Application

____ Application Description (400-500 words)

____ Application Story (400-500 words)

____ Activity Photos (1-3 photos)

____ Adult Photo Releases - Signed

____ Children Photo Releases Signed

____ Intellectual Property Release - Signed

**EMAIL US YOUR ACTIVITY THROUGH OUR WEBSITE**

# Family Wild

"*The butterfly counts not months but moments, and has time enough.*"

Rabindranath Tagore
Nobel Prize Winning Bengali Author

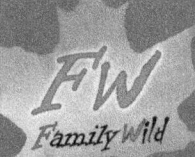

# Family Wild

## Chapter
## 4
## Wildlife Art

## Show

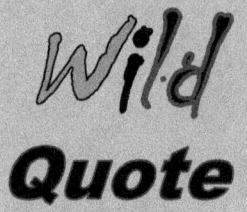

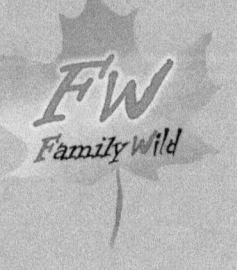

# Now What?

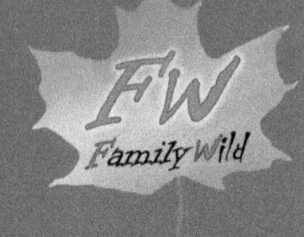

## Family Wild FUN!

You've achieved the hardest part - you started. Now what??? You need to plan your first activity.

### YOU CAN DO ANYTHING YOU WANT.

Our suggestion? Ask your membership (FAMILY) what they enjoy. Go around the room. Ask everyone what they would like to do, then make a list, make a decision and start planning. Maybe you'd like to create a new bird-feeding station in your yard, try your hand at painting or go for a nature walk and write a one-act play about your adventures.

***Can't decide?*** Have everyone write an idea on a piece of paper, then put it in a hat or bowl and blind-pick one or two. You could also ask each member gets to pick an activity and then immediately mark them all out on a calendar.

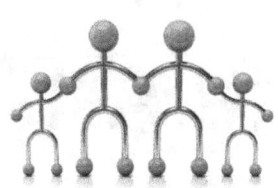

### *You may find yourself shocked by what your members suggest.*

As a child, I (Kim) remember being so full of the sounds and smells of my state forest that I needed a way to communicate what I was feeling. We had a lovely old piano in the house, a family treasure from my Grandma Harris. Although I was never very happy with music lessons, I started to put sounds together and soon was on my way to creating my own melodies. Later, I learned to facilitate drum circles so kids and adults could share what they were feeling through rhythm and voice. We all have our creative stories - share them with your kids today and listen to their own artistic yearnings. Then GO WILD!

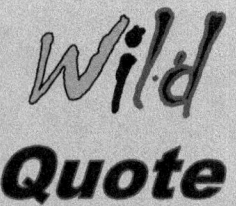
# Family Wild Art Show

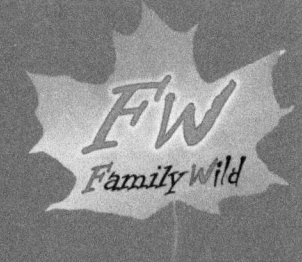

"To be

an

artist is

to

believe

in life."


**Henry Moore**
English Artist

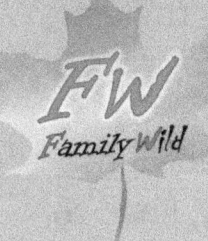

## <u>YOUR</u> Family Wild Art Shows

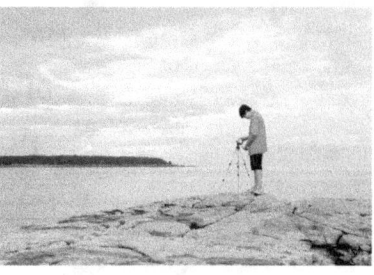

I (Mike) often mention I was a photography instructor at our local community college. At the end of each semester, the art department put on a one day art show. My students would display their images along with all the other art students. The pride you saw on the face of the students was mirrored in the smiles of their parents and family.

We created the Family Wild Arts Book to recognize those members who love to create from their Wild experiences. Many people may not care to pull a trigger or set a hook, but still love to spend time in the woods or on the water.

As with our Family Wild Tournaments, you can make your Family Wild Art Show keep your art show as small (or grow it as big) as your club wants.

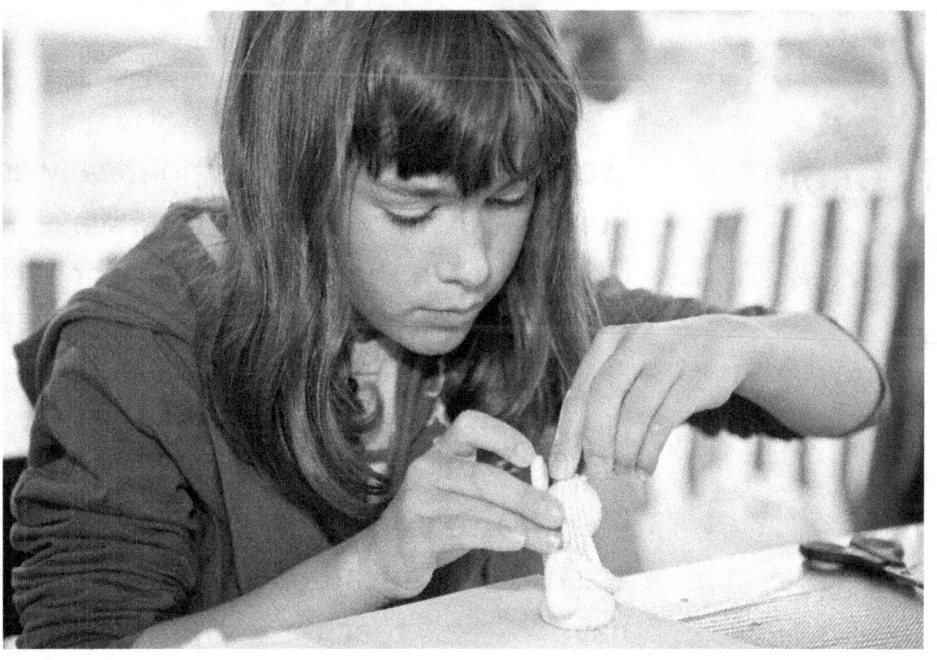

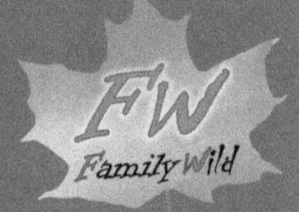

We know the idea of putting on an art show may seem overwhelming. Let me tell you a story. Our local high school asked me to teach photography to their alternative education students. Alt-Ed students are those kids challenged by life and traditional school. You can often recognize them dressed in black, with tattoos and body piercings. HA!

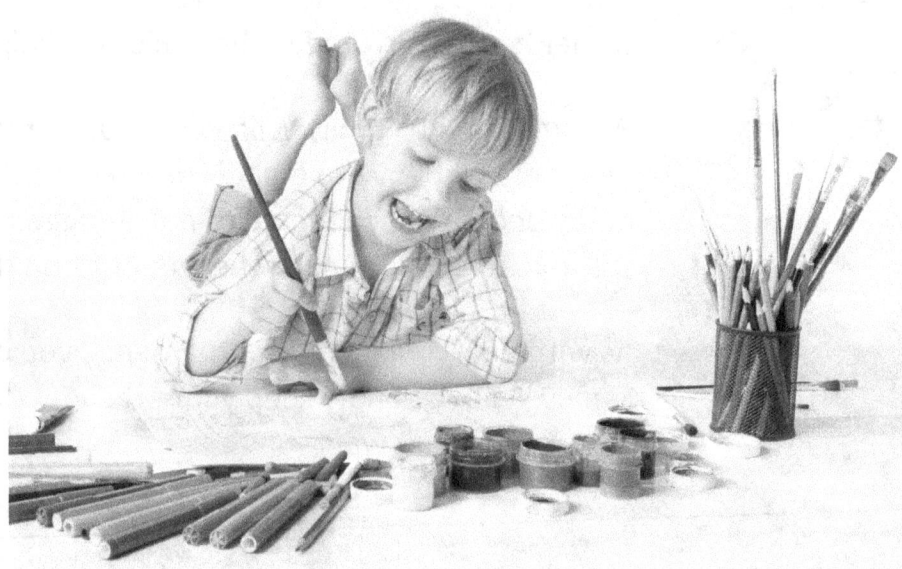

Well, let me tell you, as a politically conservative business owner, let's just say I was the minority in the classroom on that first day. As they looked at me at in the front of the class room with skeptical eyes and shiny nose rings, I said, "You all don't listen to Rush Limbaugh do you?"

Thus started my Alternative Education career. Since I wasn't an "educated" and certified teacher, I had to have a "real" teacher in the classroom with me.

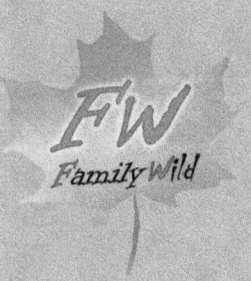

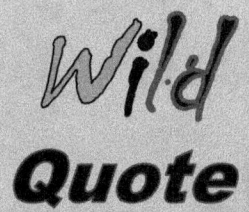
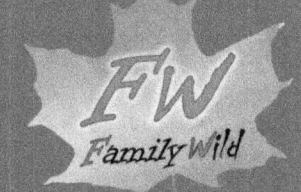
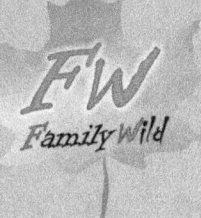
I taught that class of high schoolers exactly the way I instructed my college students. This meant we needed to host an art show. The "real" teacher told me I just didn't understand "these" students. There was NO WAY they could do an art show. We'd be lucky just to get them to "show" up for class.

Then she told me in no uncertain terms that "she"

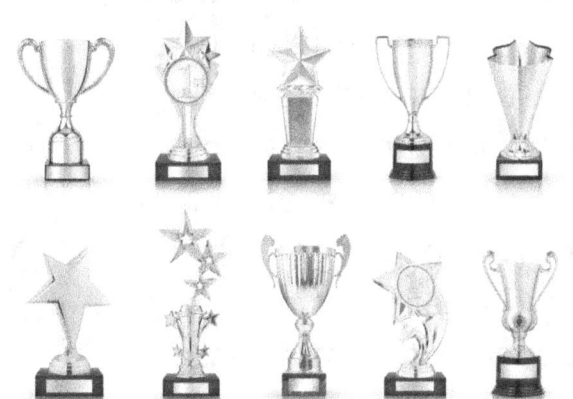

wasn't going to do anything to help put on the exhibit because it would be a waste of her time.

Well, I told her she and I would have to agree to disagree. I told her that not only would we have an Art Show at the end of the year but the students would put it on and do all the work. She rolled her eyes and walked away, knowing I was just dreaming.

There were two things I knew she *didn't* know. I knew the allure of photography and I trusted the power of students when they learn to unleash their creativity.

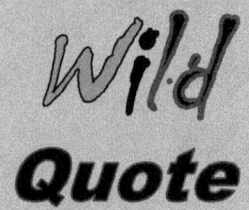

# Family Wild Art Show

## Continued

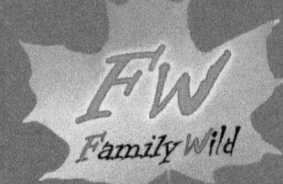

So I challenged those students just as I'll challenge you. I told them they would have to set up committees to handle the event. They would have to pick one or two people to find a location for our show. Then they would have to promote our show. Someone would have to set up the tables and art projects.

I told them I expected them to dress appropriately (their finest black outfits) and welcome our guests. They also had to designate a clean up crew for the end of the night. Finally, someone had to send out Press Releases and pictures to the news media to report our event as well as thank you notes to all the supporters of our event.

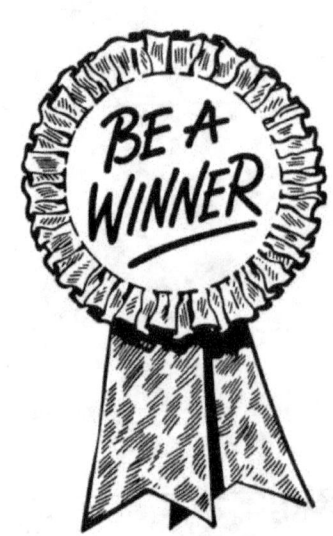

My teaching counterpart consistently reminded me throughout the semester this "show" would never happen and that I'd be sorely disappointed.

To make a long story short, we had our show at the local mall. My unique students made an appointment with the mall manager, put together a small presentation, and requested she donate space for our show.

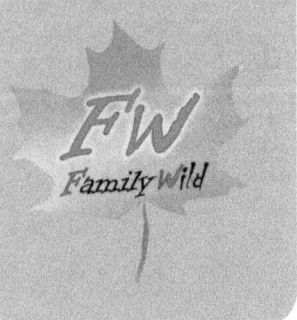

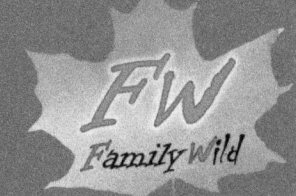

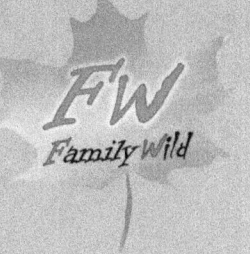

## Wild Quote

Our other committee sought and received donations for decorations and they secured the tables we needed for displays. The Public Relations Committee sent out notices to all the media and we received countless offers for free advertising for our event.

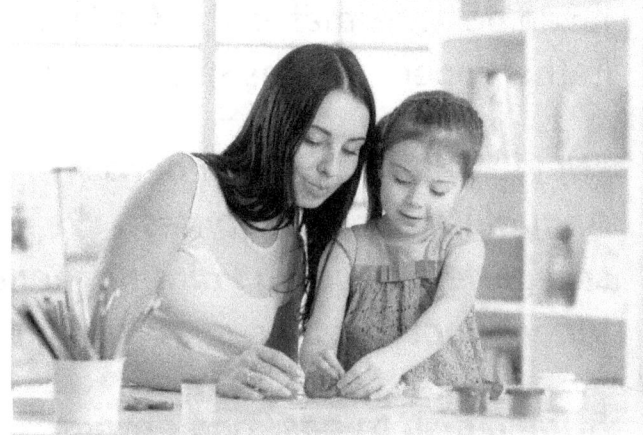

The night of the show, every single alternative education student showed up on time, set up the show and greeted our guests professionally. Just as with my college students, these high schoolers beamed with pride as family, friends and strangers walked through their display.

At the end of the night, they cleaned up our show. Every one of them walked with a new air of confidence as they enjoyed the fruits of their labors. The next day, out went the "thank-you" letters and press releases.

I tell you this story because your Family Wild Club is only a bit of imagination and some adult direction away from creating your own Family Wild Art Show to celebrate the works of your membership.

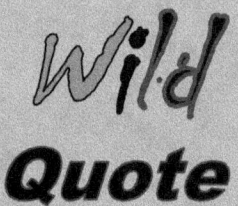
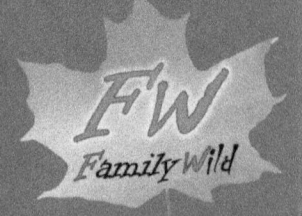
Your Art Show doesn't have to be at a Mall nor does it even need to be a public event. You can hold it in a home, at camp, or at a park. For your first event, you may want to keep it small and just for immediate family and friends.

It can be as formal as the Art Show Announcement in the Appendix or as simple as below:

*"Hey! Saturday, September 19th, come to our First Annual Wildlife Art Contest. We'll have several categories including Painting, Pencil Drawing, Video, Photography and Writing.*

*Bring a dish to pass and prepare yourselves for a ton of fun. Think about it! When hasn't food made for a better event?!"*

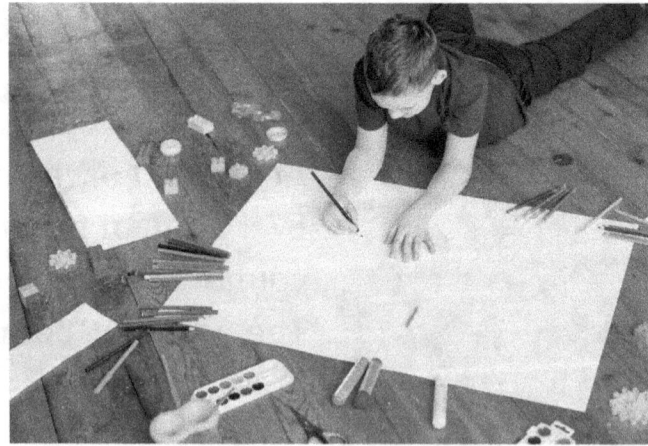

A simple invitation stands between you and your family, friends (or your entire town if you want) making memories! Again, design an event as big or small as you want.

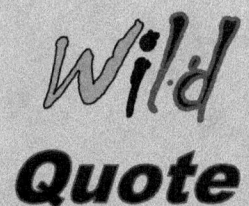

# Family Wild Art Show

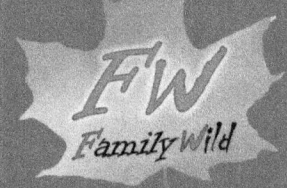

## Continued

## <u>YOUR</u> Family Wild Art Show
## <u>Who, What, Where,</u>
## <u>When, Why and How?"</u>

**Your** art show so your rules. The *size* of the event will determine *how detailed you want* to structure your event. I always recommend the **5 W's:** Who, What, Where, When, Why and then I add in the H-How?

**Who** - who do you want in your art show? Do you want to have a contest? How do you want to determine the winners of the

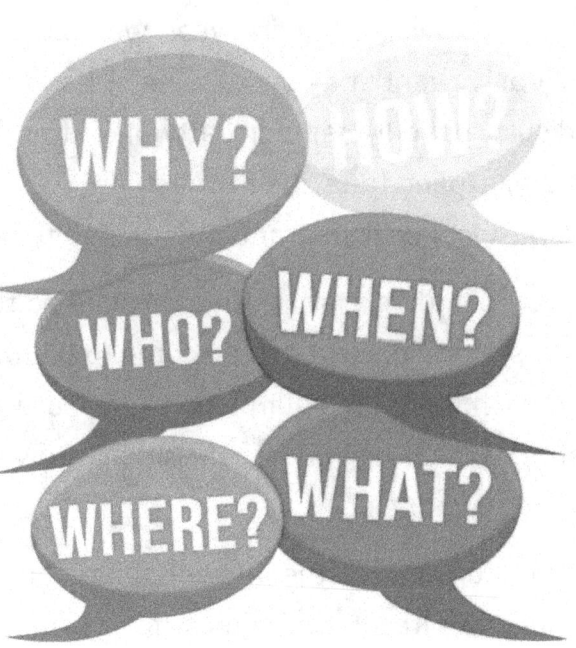

contest? Maybe you just want to display the works of art, which is just fine.

Remember, the goal is to HAVE FUN! The more displays you have, the more fun everyone will enjoy. Encourage ALL of your members to produce a piece of art for the show.

Adults can get in the act, too. In fact, we strongly encourage you to participate as more than just a guest. If adults take the chance and put forth their artwork, it will add a further level of credibility and excitement for your younger members.

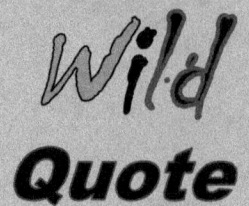
# Family Wild Art Show

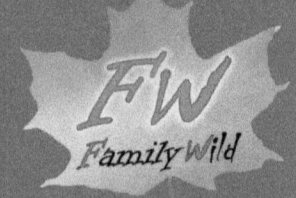

## Continued

**What** - What shall we display? What committees do we need? What do we expect each committee to do for the art show? What do we need to put on the show? What size do we want the show?

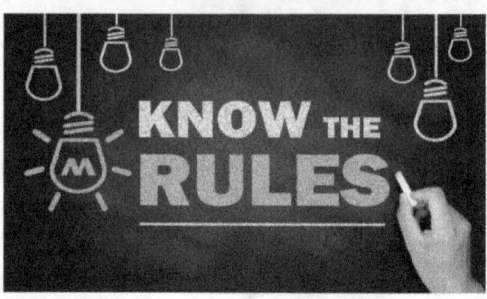

## *Don't ever limit your WHAT when it comes to your art shows!*

**Where -** The size of your show will determine where you want to host your show. For the first year, we recommend you start with a family-only event at a house, cabin or park. You'll still need tables for display of your members' artwork. After the first year, don't be afraid to expand the size of your show. You might approach a local mall, business or restaurant and ask if they can host your event.

The key to finding a great venue? You need to emphasize the benefits of having new people come to their business to your potential host. Share your plans to promote your event and your intentions of putting on a professional show of wildlife art projects created by your club.

Don't underestimate the power of an organized club requesting a partnership with a local business for mutual benefit. Remember, a business needs customers and traffic flow and you can provide a whole new stream of people for the business and, the best part, at no cost to the business or you.

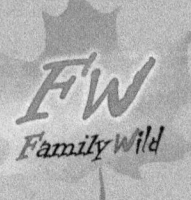

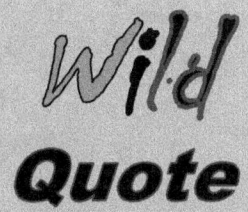

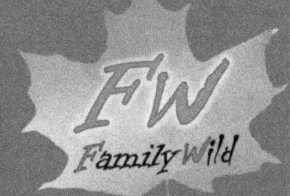

**When** - "When" varies much more than you think! When you ask yourself "when", think about a couple of things. First, think of your Art Show as an annual event. In other words, you should know your date for this year, and the next and the next. If you schedule your event this year for Saturday, July 10th, which happens to fall on the second Saturday of July this year, make sure to let everyone know that future events will always occur on the second Saturday of July.

If you're really on the ball, make sure you have a flyer ready to

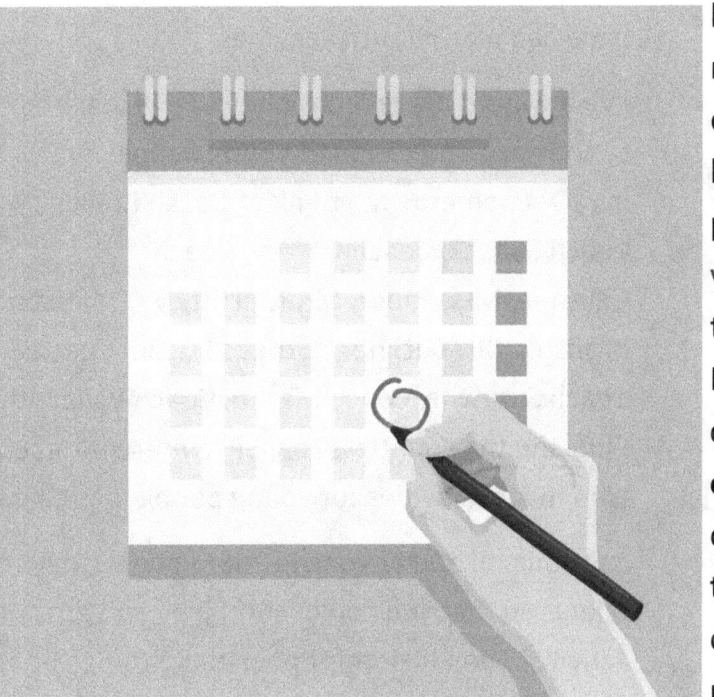

hand out for next year's event. What better way to promote next year's tournament?!! In fact, **give everyone 5 extra flyers** and challenge them to bring at least one new participant next year! You might even give out a certificate for the person who brings the most new artists next year.

Many folks have to set their vacation schedules in December or January and want to know special dates well in advance so they can make sure they can attend in the future. We've found it takes three years to truly establish a show.

"Creativity

is piercing

the

mundane to

find the

marvelous."

**Daniel
Patrick
Moynihan**
American
Politician

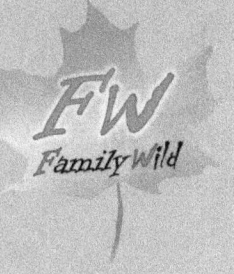

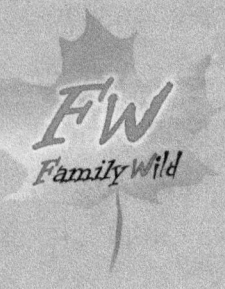

# Family Wild Art Show

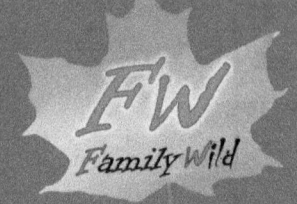

## Continued

**Why -** "Why" would you ever want to commit yourself or your family to hours of planning, preparation, calling, texting, reminding, getting up hours earlier than anyone else, and staying hours after to clean up after your show??? Great questions!

I (Mike) grew up as the worst player on pretty much every sports team on which I ever played. You know, the chubby kid that couldn't run, couldn't skate, couldn't hit, shoot or dribble, but loved to play and be on a team with the guys. As an adult, I realized that without the adult mentors, we wouldn't have had many youth activities.

I've always felt a responsibility to give back to the next generation of young people. In my own hometown, I think of Coach Rohn, Coach Sobeck, Coach Hassey, Coach Gillespie, Mrs. Taber, Mr. Merritt, Mr. Mattson, Mr. Bray, Mr. Bronson, Mr. Buckner, "Stripes" Gillin, Coach Froggett, Coach Fisher, Coach Susewitz, Coach Martin, Coach Vivian, the Alpena Boosters Club and the countless coaches, referees, teachers and fundraisers who made activities for young people possible.

Ask yourself, did anyone in your younger days donate their time and talents so that you could learn, play and grow in a youth-based activity? Then take this opportunity to pay homage to your memory of their impact on your life.

Tip your hat to your coaches, your teachers, and mentors and invest hours of your time and your talents in making your Family Wild memories possible for the enjoyment of all! Heck, maybe someday you'll write a book just so you can list their names as another way of saying thank you!

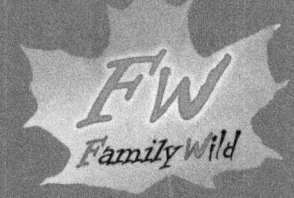
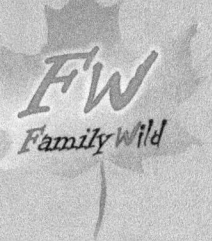
**How** - We end with HOW you do this because it follows Who, What, Where, When and Why - you know, the easy questions. Now comes the hard part. HOW will we get this done???

Have you heard the old and famous Chinese proverb *"A journey of a thousand miles begins with one step?"* You'll find this holds true with everything in life and especially your Family Wild activities.

Your expectations hold the key to successfully completing the HOW? You and your club not only get to decide how you do things but you get to learn from everything you didn't like at the end of the day and can improve upon it next year.

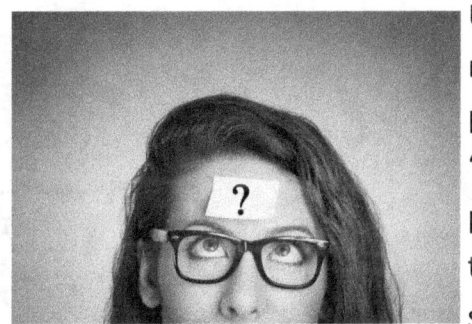

Usually, every club has that great note taker, or better yet, the person who seems to have all the "constructive criticisms" for pretty much everything! Ask them to tally all the thoughts, suggestions, problems and results from the event.

At the **VERY NEXT MEETING** review this as a club. Decide what to keep for next year, what to do different and what to dump all together. We guarantee if you follow this advice, your events will not only improve but continue to grow.

Remember to remind everyone during the meeting that suggestions or critiques aren't meant to hurt people, but rather, serve as constructive ways to make everyone's experience better. President Harry S. Truman once said "It is amazing what you can accomplish **IF** you do not care who gets the credit." We suggest you make that a creed of all your **Family Wild** activities.

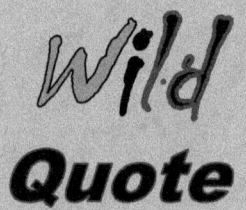
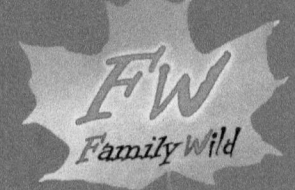
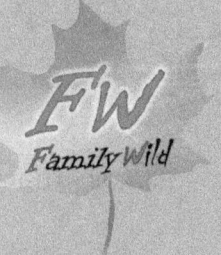
## Certificates / Trophies

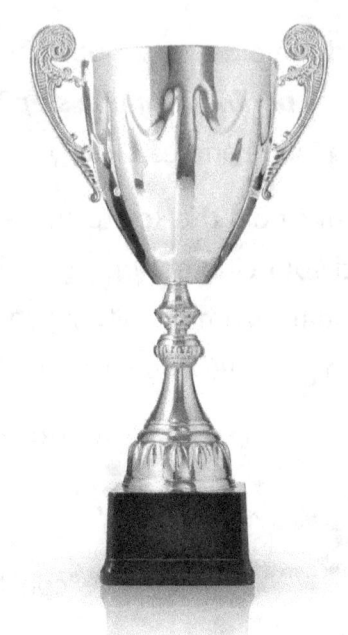

The energy of your entire event must come from the energy of the organizers - **YOU!!!** One of the easiest ways to create that excitement is to recognize the achievements of your artists. You don't have to spend a ton of money on such recognition, but make sure to do it.

As you gather everyone before your show, announce the divisions, categories, age brackets, and make sure you display your certificates or trophies for everyone to see.

You don't have to spend a ton of money on your awards. Think outside the box. For instance, make your own trophies and ask your younger members to help. You might also ask friends for "hand-me-down" trophies that can be repurposed.

Put the word out on Facebook and ask for donations. You may find yourself with more trophies than you can use. Remember, you just want to recognize the achievements of young and old alike in a fun and memorable way.

Consider starting with certificates and working your way up. You can always expand to store-bought trophies as your tournament grows. Prioritize the size of the *Family Wild* "FUN" not the trophy. See the **Appendix** for examples.

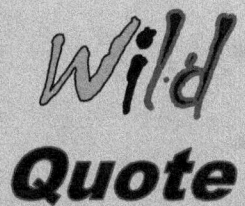
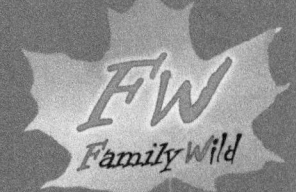
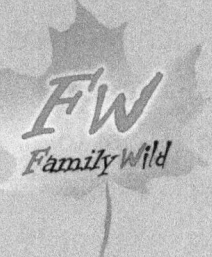
# Promotion

The size of your event will determine your promotional needs. If you want to keep it in the family, an email or letter will work. IF you chose to make it larger, consider posters and flyers.

You can take them to sporting goods stores, post them on community boards, drop them off to clubs and organizations like the Boys and Girls Clubs, Boy Scouts, schools, Senior Citizen Centers, etc.

Also, reach out to local hunting, fishing and art clubs and non-profit organizations (Kiwanis or Rotary for example) as sponsors and a great place to find volunteers. You may consider "piggybacking" an existing event and offer to run a new Wildlife and Nature Art Show division. We've found helping to make an existing event better benefits everyone.

Also, don't fear traditional promotional avenues like radio and TV. See an example of a *Public Service Announcement (PSA)/Press Release* in the Appendix.

Distribute PSA's and Press Releases in person, by mail, or e-mail to television and radio stations, newspapers, hunting/fishing/art shows, wherever you can promote your event. Think as big as you want, but keep it manageable and keep it *Family Wild* fun. Trust us, it will grow!

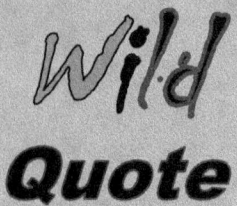
# Family Wild Art Shows

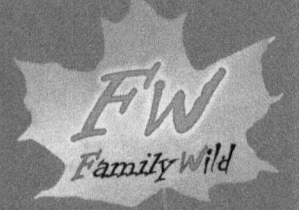

## Continued

**Facebook Page** - If you have a young computer-savvy Family Wild member, challenge them to create a permanent Facebook page to communicate the progress and results of your events and club. Let your young members manage the page with your assistance.

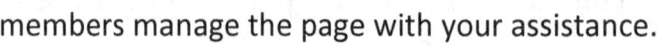

Imagine you've just finished your first event. Now what?

## PROMOTE YOUR RESULTS!!!

Regardless of the size of your event, make the time to celebrate your winners and your art show. Send out emails announcing your participants or winners, post it on Facebook and send out press releases to the local media. Also, make sure you invite your local TV station news media to cover your event and awards ceremony. The smaller the station, the more likely they'll cover your story. Imagine the worst that could happen if you invite media or other dignitaries. They could say no. On the other hand, they might say YES!!!

You'll LOVE the FREE advertising and news coverage of your event.

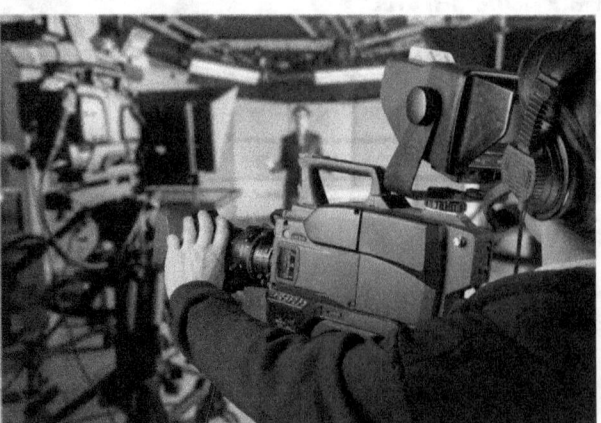

More importantly, so will your family of competitors. Again, don't worry about the size of your event. Let the media decide whether or not to cover your **Family Wild** Tournament.

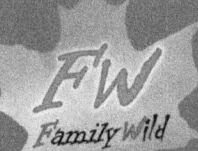

# Family Wild

## Chapter

## 5

## Artist Club

## Membership

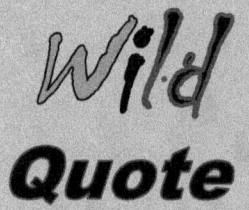

# Artist Club Award

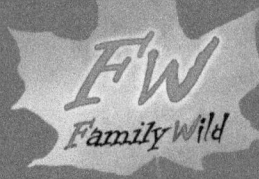

## Family Wild

When you try a form of art for the first time, you join the group that started with cavemen drawing on walls to Leonardo DaVinci and Picasso to today's Wildlife TV Shows. Our Artist Club encourages you to try all of the arts while you enjoy the outdoors.

You don't HAVE to pull a trigger or set a hook to enjoy Family Wild projects and our great natural resources. Just as with a first successful hunting or fishing adventure, your members can earn entry into the Family Wild Artist Club with their first successful artistic attempt.

The only thing we ask is that the subject depicts wildlife or the outdoors. You can also include members of your Family Wild club.

Look for future Family Wild Art Contests at our Family Wild website and submit your projects. We hope you enjoy earning your Slams, beginning with earning your membership into the Family Wild Artist Club!

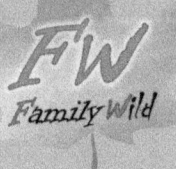

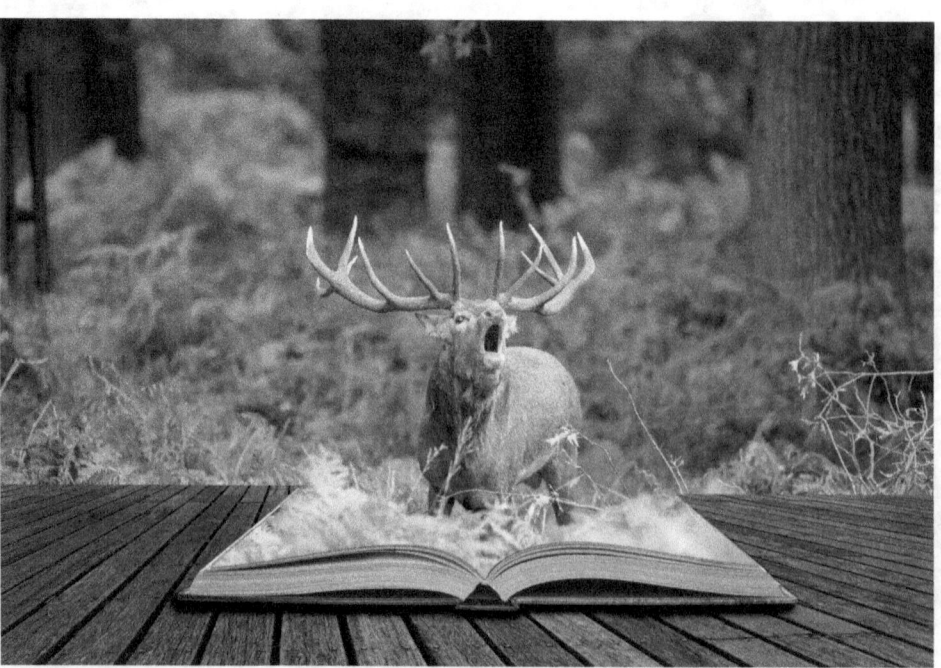

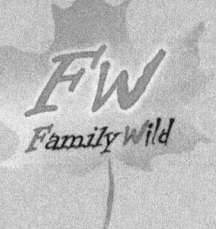
# Family Wild Art Log

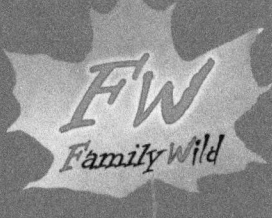

At the end of each Slam description, we've placed *Family Wild* Art Logs to document your successful art adventure. Make the time and take the time to record memories with your young artist.

You may want to purchase a *Family Wild* Art Slam Journal for each of your fishermen so they can individually record their personal lifetime of memories. These are much less expensive than our full manuals and can be personalized to the individual.

Logs and diaries have conveyed critical North American history over the past two hundred years. Understand that the Lewis & Clark journals told a nation about the new West, not to mention inspiring generations who continue to read them.

Also, we encourage you to take LOTS of pictures - start a scrapbook. Send them to us via our webpage at

## www.familywildprogram.com.

Today's pictures are tomorrow's treasures. We've even included space in your log area to glue a couple photos.

You'll have fun documenting your adventures in your logs as a part of the requirements to earn your Slams and 50 years from now your young artists grandchildren will find them priceless.

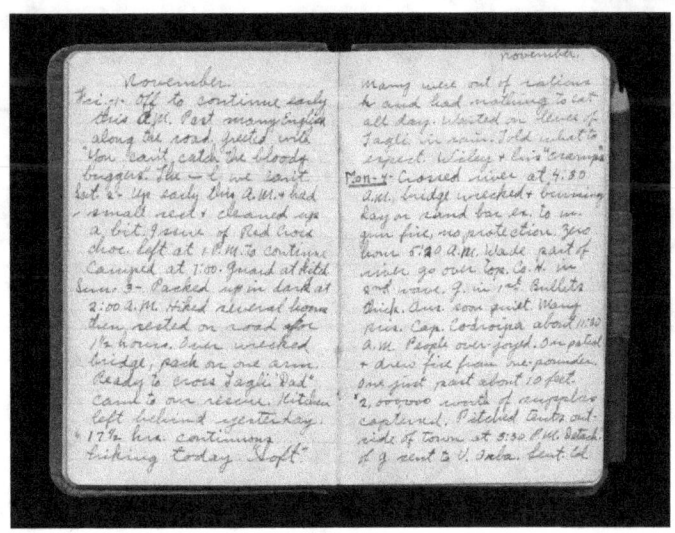

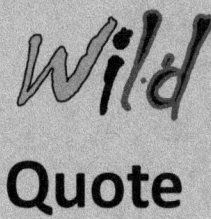

# Wild
## Quote

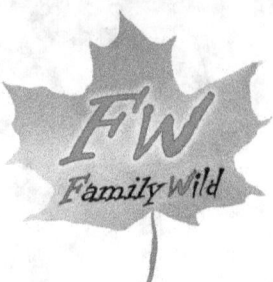

"Difficult

roads

often

lead to

beautiful

destinations."

## Author Unknown

## Family Wild Log

Member Name_____

Date_____ Time _____

Member's Age _____ Location _____

Art Project _____

Art Medium Used _____

Wildlife or Nature Included

_____

_____

_____

Family Wild Members involved (names)

_____

_____

_____

Special Memories _____

_____

_____

_____

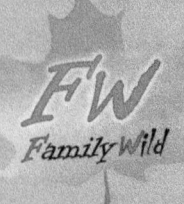

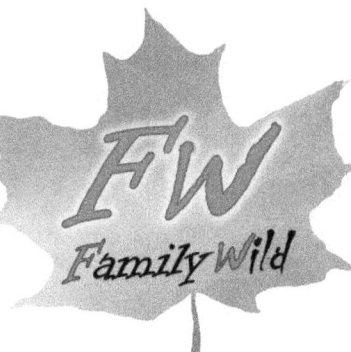

# Family Wild

*Herby certifies that*

_____

*Earned FamilyWild's*

# Artist Club Membership

| | |
|---|---|
| **Date** _____ | **Project** _____ |
| **Place** _____ | |
| **Working with** _____ | |

_____

*FamilyWild Local Chapter President*

*Michael Nunneley*

*FamilyWild National President*

# SLAM PICTURES

## Glue a couple pictures here

## to remember your SLAM!

You can keep the pictures in your book or put them
on the back of your certificate in a frame to
commemorate your art work!

**Below, take a few minutes to tell your story in your own words.**

Think of it as telling your grandchildren about your
art experience. It will be like sending a post card to
someone who will read it 50-100 years from now!

## My Slam Story

_____

_____

_____

_____

_____

_____

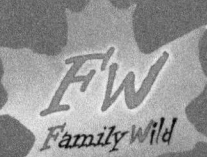

# Family Wild

## Chapter
## 6
## Family Wild
## Art Slams

# Family Wild Art Slam

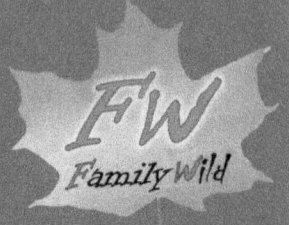

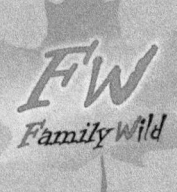
We've created a series of Outdoor Art challenges we call Art Slams. For your young artists to earn these Slams, they'll spend hours practicing, preparing and learning from their parents/grandparents, mentors, books and internet sources about all the things it takes to become successful artists.

Most of the Slams require the artists to create at least three art projects with the media suggested. On our website, you'll find Free Art Slam Certificates you can give to acknowledge their artistic accomplishments.

Make a **BIG** deal out of your young artist earning each of these Slams. Not everyone is born to be a hunter or fisherman, but that doesn't mean they can't enjoy the outdoors. In fact, we DARE YOU to try and earn your own *Family Wild Art* Slams along-side your youngsters!

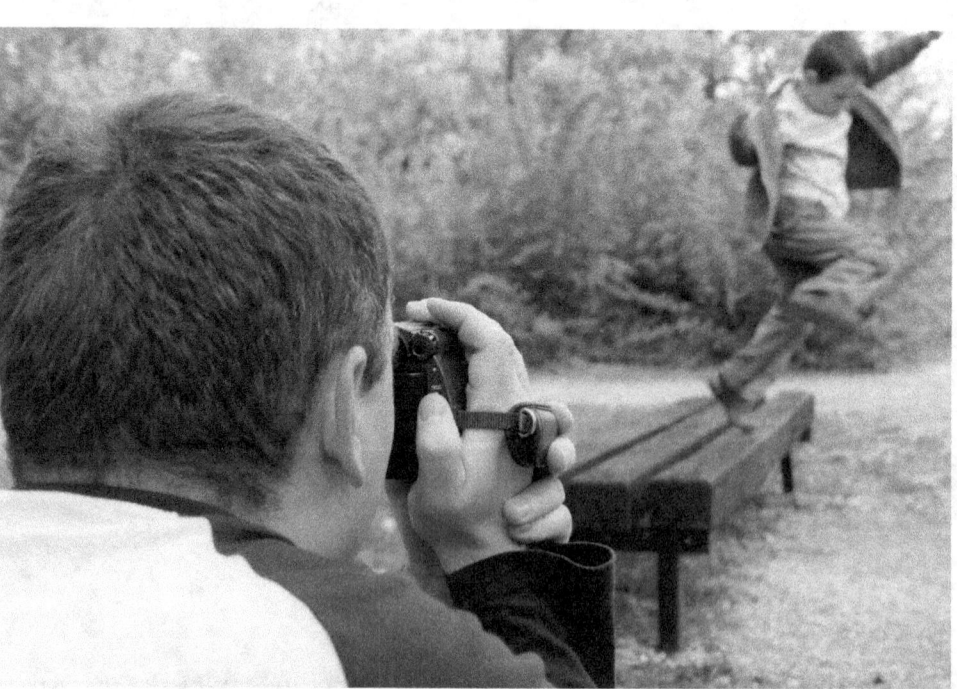

*"Hunting, fishing, drawing, and music occupied my every moment. Cares I knew not, and cared naught about them."*

**James John Audubon**
American Ornithologist & Painter

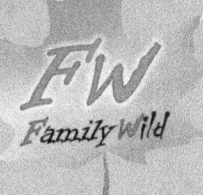

# Art Slams

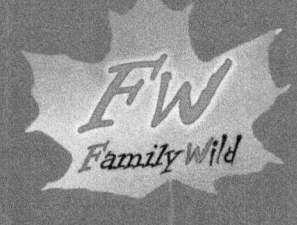

## Objective – Get Family Wild !

Slam Awards celebrate your family member's art achievements. All of our Family Wild Slams challenge our members to persevere to truly earn their certificates not just get "participation" awards. We challenge you to **CHALLENGE THEM!!!**

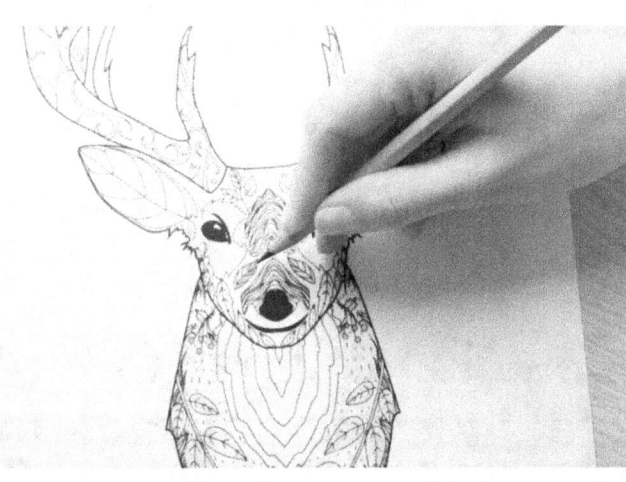

Art doesn't just happen by luck. It often takes hours of practice, trying, trying again. Make sure you encourage your young artist to create the best project they can as they earn their Slams.

We have tried to make our Slams challenging but attainable. Remember, with our Art Slams we require 3 projects for each theme. Try to be there to help your young artist but not too much. Let them try wild new things that might roll your more "adult" eyes. Have fun with it.

**AGAIN**, we beg you, don't make this easy on your young artists! At Family Wild we don't make a habit of handing out awards just to make everyone feel good about themselves.

Hunting and fishing combine failure and success and Art is no different. Everyone can hunt, fish and create art - hard workers get to "harvest", "catch" and "create" too!

Earning a Family Wild Slam symbolizes what it took to achieve success in a **Family Wild** sort of way!!!

# *Family Wild*

"Success is not final, failure is not fatal, it is the courage to continue that counts."

**Winston Churchill**
British Prime
Minister

# Writing Slams

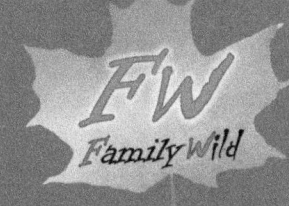

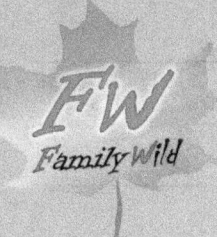

FW
Family Wild

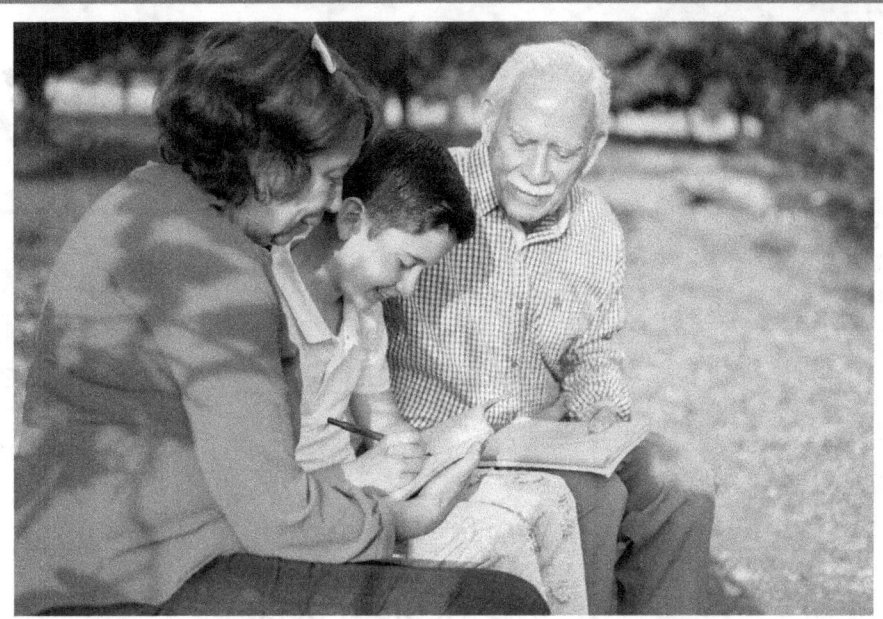

Many young people (of all ages) enjoy writing. Using words to describe all the senses, thoughts and feelings of being outdoors can ease the mind and the soul. I still spend about twenty minutes a day writing in my journal, capturing the changes in weather, animals and plant life I see. Sometimes a poem will spring to life during that period, which is an added "sprinkle" on my daily donut.

Writing is one of the best ways to wake up and actually notice what is around and within you, one of the "paths" I've used since I was in elementary school. It's also one of those life skills that will stay with you through all your educational and working experiences. In this age of texting and hurry-up social media, it's also a craft that deserves preservation!

To earn the Writing Slam, you need to create one of the following with an outdoor, animal, bird or fish theme: Essay, News Article, Internet-Based Writing, Blog, Interviews, Poetry, Journaling, Play/Script, Short Stories, Comics.

As you can see, only a pen or keyboard and your young author's imagination stand in the way of earning a Family Wild Writing Slam. In a way, this Slam is how Family Wild got started!

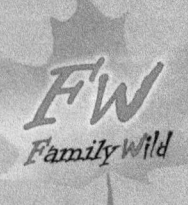

# Writing Project 1

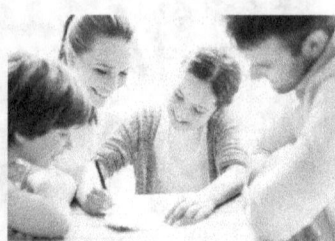

## Family Wild Log

Member Name_____

Date_____ Time _____

Member's Age _____ Location _____

Art Project _____

Art Medium Used _____

Wildlife or Nature Included

_____

_____

_____

Family Wild Members involved (names)

_____

_____

_____

Special Memories _____

_____

_____

_____

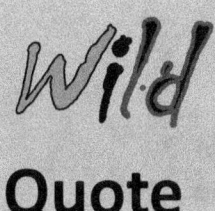

# Writing Project #2

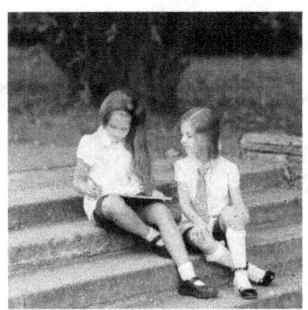

## Family Wild Log

Member Name_____

Date_____ Time _____

Member's Age _____ Location _____

Art Project _____

Art Medium Used _____

Wildlife or Nature Included

_____

_____

_____

Family Wild Members involved (names)

_____

_____

_____

Special Memories _____

_____

_____

_____

_____

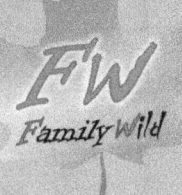

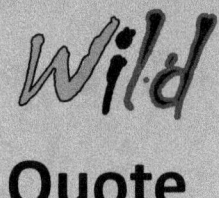
**Writing Project #3**

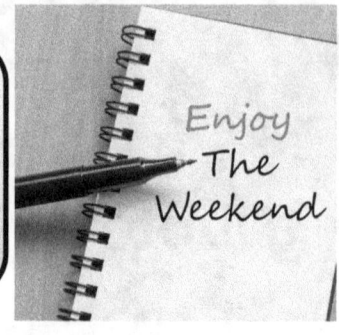

Enjoy The Weekend

# *Family Wild Log*

"It's not just about creativity. It's about the person you are becoming *while* you are creating."

## Charlie Peacock
American Singer

Member Name_____

Date_____ Time _____

Member's Age _____ Location _____

Art Project _____

Art Medium Used _____

Wildlife or Nature Included

_____

_____

_____

Family Wild Members involved (names)

_____

_____

_____

Special Memories _____

_____

_____

_____

_____

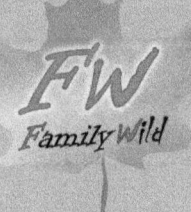

FW
*Family Wild*

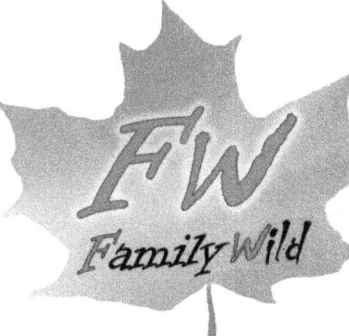

# Family Wild

*Herby certifies that*

_____

*Earned FamilyWild's*

# Writing Slam

Date _____    Project_____

Date _____    Project_____

Date _____    Project_____

_____    *Michael Nunneley*

*FamilyWild Local Chapter President*    *FamilyWild National President*

# SLAM PICTURES

## Glue a couple pictures here

## to remember your SLAM!

You can keep the pictures in your book or put them
on the back of your certificate in a frame to
commemorate your art work!

**Below, take a few minutes to tell your story in your own words.**

Think of it as telling your grandchildren about your
art experience. It will be like sending a post card to
someone who will read it 50-100 years from now!

# My Slam Story

_____

_____

_____

_____

_____

_____

_____

# Drawing Slam

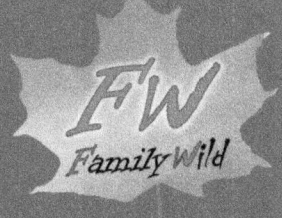

"Earth

without

'art' is

just

'eh'."

**Author Unknown**

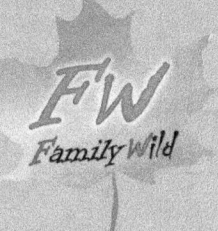

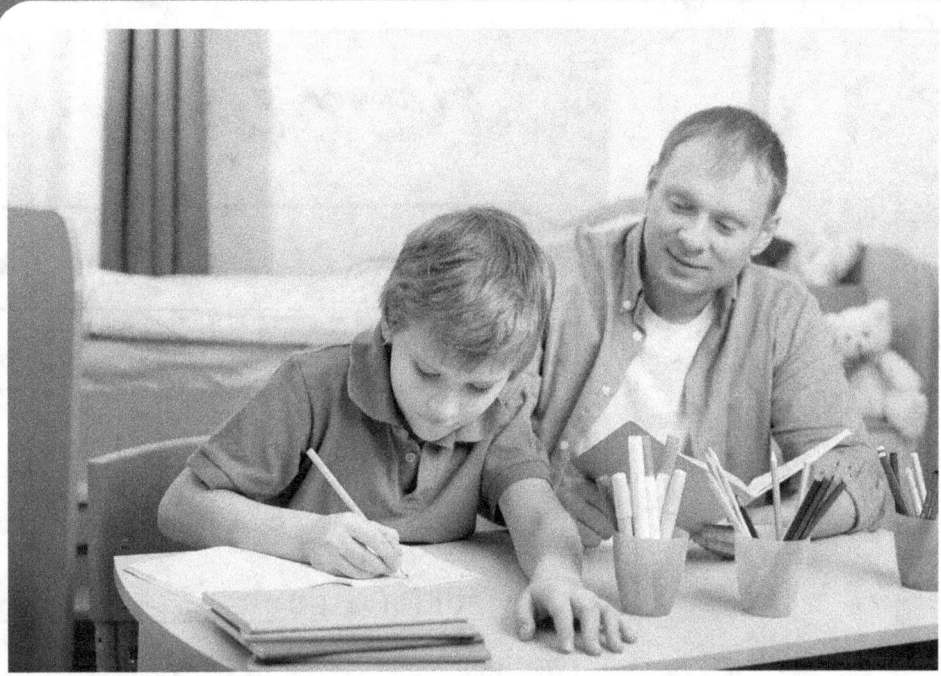

Thank goodness for photography, because personally I couldn't draw stick figures, but I know many people young and old whose drawings look like photographs.

We ask that you create at least three different wildlife drawings using a different medium for each. You can chose from pen/ink, pencil, colored pencil, charcoal, pastels, crayon or even our Family Wild Coloring Books.

As you can see, your members have an enormous selection of mediums try as they create their outdoor expressions. Don't be too critical of their attempts and make sure to encourage trying as many as they'd like. We do want three distinct drawings as a final product.

If they only want to draw a deer for example that's fine. One could be in a field, one could be a fall setting and another along a stream, each with different looking animal. The idea is to challenge them in a Wild sort of way!

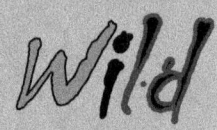

# Wild
## Quote

"The worse enemy of creativity is self-doubt."

## Sylvia Plath
American Writer

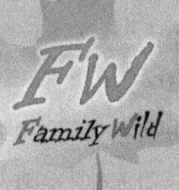

FW
Family Wild

## Drawing Project #1

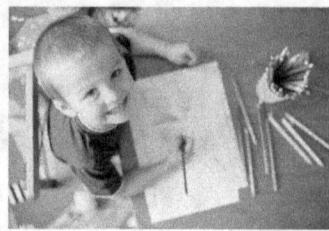

# Family Wild Log

Member Name _____

Date _____ Time _____

Member's Age _____ Location _____

Art Project _____

Art Medium Used _____

Wildlife or Nature Included

_____

_____

_____

Family Wild Members involved (names)

_____

_____

_____

Special Memories _____

_____

_____

_____

_____

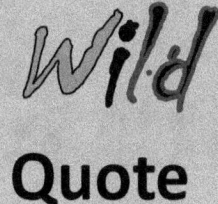

# Wild

## Quote

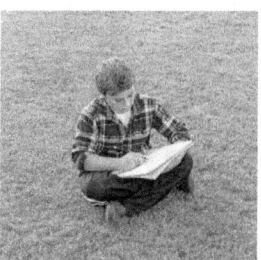

*Family Wild Log*

"Blessed are

the curious

for they

shall have

adventures."

**Author
Unknown**

**FW**
*Family Wild*

Member Name_____

Date_____ Time _____

Member's Age _____ Location _____

Art Project _____

Art Medium Used _____

Wildlife or Nature Included

_____

_____

_____

Family Wild Members involved (names)

_____

_____

_____

Special Memories _____

_____

_____

_____

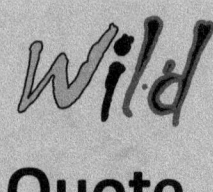
Drawing
Project #3

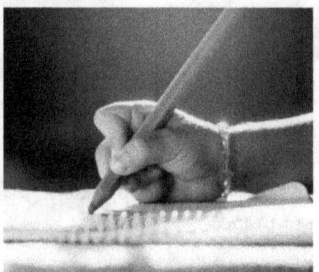

*Family Wild Log*

"Thinking

here "goes

nothing"

could be the

start of

everything."

**Drew
Wagner**
Writer

Member Name_____

Date_____ Time _____

Member's Age _____ Location _____

Art Project _____

Art Medium Used _____

Wildlife or Nature Included

_____

_____

_____

Family Wild Members involved (names)

_____

_____

_____

Special Memories _____

_____

_____

_____

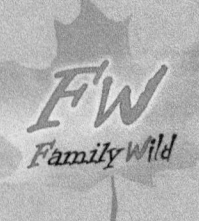

FW
Family Wild

# *SLAM PICTURES*

## *Glue a couple pictures here*

## *to remember your SLAM!*

You can keep the pictures in your book or put them
on the back of your certificate in a frame to
commemorate your art work!

**Below, take a few minutes to tell your story in your own words.**

Think of it as telling your grandchildren about your
art experience. It will be like sending a post card to
someone who will read it 50-100 years from now!

## My Slam Story

_____

_____

_____

_____

_____

_____

_____

# MORE SLAM PICTURES

## Glue a couple pictures here
## to remember your SLAM.

You can keep the pictures in your book or put them on the
back of your certificate in a frame
to commemorate your art work years from now.

**Below - take a few minutes and tell your SLAM STORY.**

Think of it as telling the story to
your grandchildren some day. Do it in your own words
and handwriting - like you're sending a post card to
someone 50-100 years from now.

# MORE SLAM PICTURES

## Glue a couple pictures here
## to remember your SLAM.

You can keep the pictures in your book or put them on the
back of your certificate in a frame
to commemorate your art work years from now.

**Below - take a few minutes and tell your SLAM STORY.**

Think of it as telling the story to
your grandchildren some day. Do it in your own words
and handwriting - like you're sending a post card to
someone 50-100 years from now.

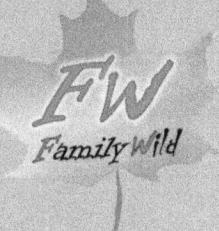
# Painting Slam

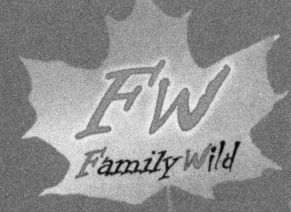

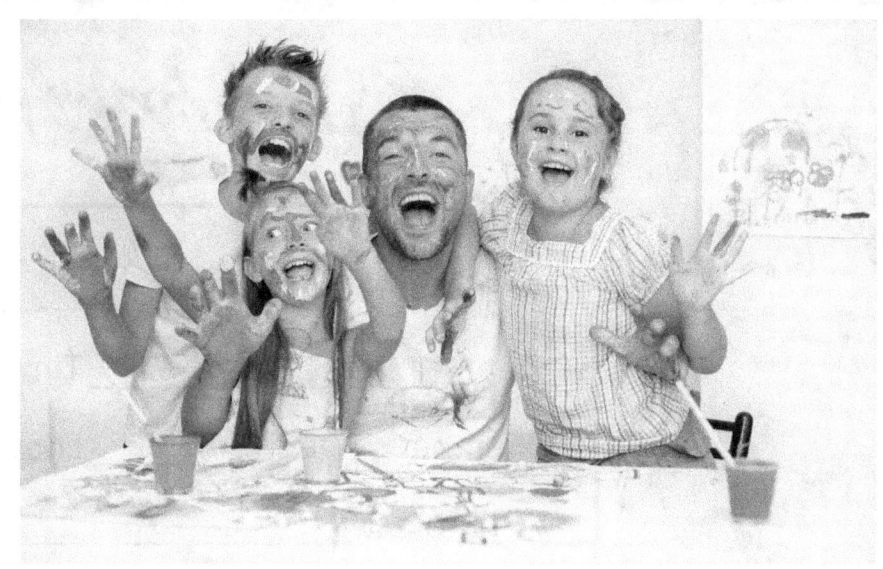

When you think of a Master Artist, you usually list the great painters of ages past. Encourage your members to try their hand at this timeless and colorful expression of art. If you don't know where to start, pursue YouTube for ideas and tips.

Your painter can chose from watercolors, oils, acrylics, ink washes and multimedia works to achieve this Slam. We encourage both adults and children to each give this a try. In my parents' house hang the paintings and drawings of each of their "grandchildren artists" — masterpieces, framed for all to see. They have become some of our family's most cherished possessions.

I (Kim) remember starting with paint-by-number kits. The love affair with color, form and the present moment aliveness of painting continues to this day. I recently created acrylic and rubbing alcohol tiles to "highlight" and add color to my home.

Play with painting on different objects like a walking stick or rocks or drift wood. These surfaces work great for beginners because they aren't so formal and the creations can become part of your gardens or nature walks with just a good coat of acrylic clear coat.

## Painting Project #1

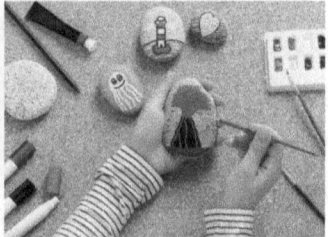

# Family Wild Log

Member Name_____

Date_____ Time _____

Member's Age _____ Location _____

Art Project _____

Art Medium Used _____

Wildlife or Nature Included

_____

_____

_____

Family Wild Members involved (names)

_____

_____

_____

Special Memories _____

_____

_____

_____

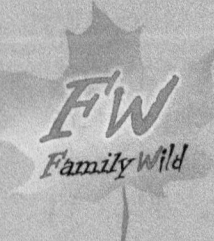

FW
Family Wild

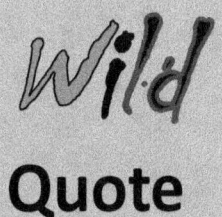
**Painting Project #2**

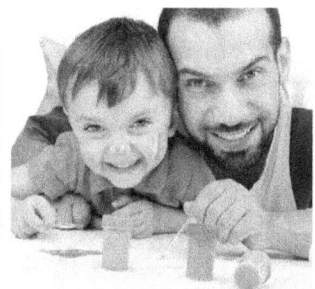

*Family Wild Log*

Member Name_____

Date_____ Time _____

Member's Age _____ Location _____

Art Project _____

Art Medium Used _____

Wildlife or Nature Included

_____

_____

_____

Family Wild Members involved (names)

_____

_____

_____

Special Memories _____

_____

_____

_____

_____

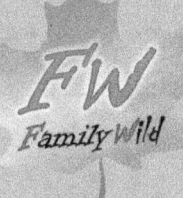

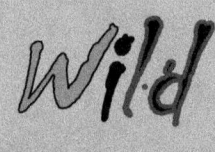

## Wild

### Quote

"Almost everything will work again if you unplug it for a few minutes… including you."

**Anne Lamott**
American Novelist

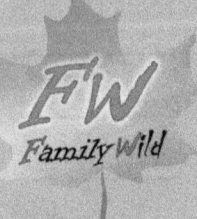
Family Wild

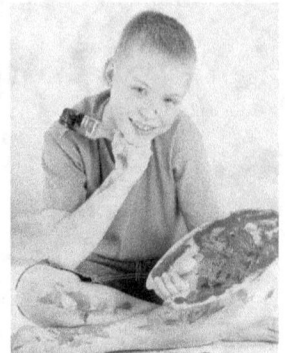

## Painting Project #3

# Family Wild Log

Member Name_____

Date_____ Time _____

Member's Age _____ Location _____

Art Project _____

Art Medium Used _____

Wildlife or Nature Included

_____

_____

_____

Family Wild Members involved (names)

_____

_____

_____

Special Memories _____

_____

_____

_____

_____

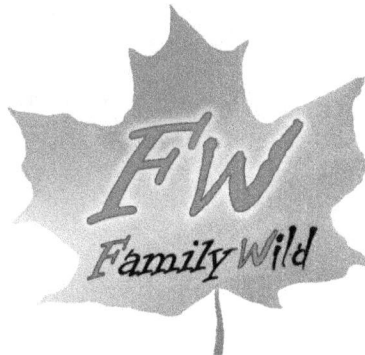

# Family Wild

*Herby certifies that*

_____

## Earned Family Wild's

# Painter Slam

| | |
|---|---|
| **Date** _____ | **Project** _____ |
| **Date** _____ | **Project** _____ |
| **Date** _____ | **Project** _____ |
| | |
| _____ | *Michael Nunneley* |
| *Family Wild Local Chapter President* | *Family Wild National President* |

# SLAM PICTURES

## Glue a couple pictures here

## to remember your SLAM!

You can keep the pictures in your book or put them
on the back of your certificate in a frame to
commemorate your art work!

**Below, take a few minutes to tell your story in your own words.**

Think of it as telling your grandchildren about your
art experience. It will be like sending a post card to
someone who will read it 50-100 years from now!

# My Slam Story

_____

_____

_____

_____

_____

_____

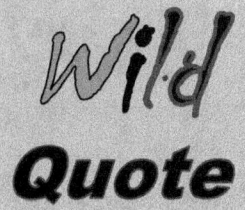
# Sculpting Slam

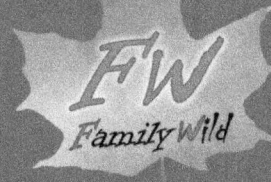
FW Family Wild

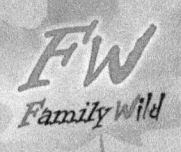
For years, in my parents' house sat a clay sculpture of a great *Boone & Crockett* level eight-point buck perched on a bookcase. Actually, it started out as a buck and ended up as a doe jumping over a log. Sadly, most people thought it was an ugly cow or dog and few saw the artistic creativity of that doe. As a result, I didn't pursue a career in sculpting but I did try. HA!

Kim wants to create wire-based frames to Paper Mache and paint and put outdoors. Because of the light nature of this kind of sculpting, you can design full sized animals, birds or even dinosaurs! Or perhaps create sitting benches using a couple of garage sale wooden chairs, attach boards as seats, then paint or add pebble and smooth art glass to mosaic to them. So even if you can't make a deer look like a deer quite yet, here are many ways to work in three dimensions as you explore this slam.

All we ask is that you try three varieties of sculpting to earn your slam. Your members can attempt clay, wood, Paper Mache, Plaster of Paris, Plaster of Paris Track Casting, Metal, or Stone.

No one would have ever confused my clay works with the high art, but I can say I tried and had a lot of fun. We hope you have a Wild time while you try your hand at sculpting!

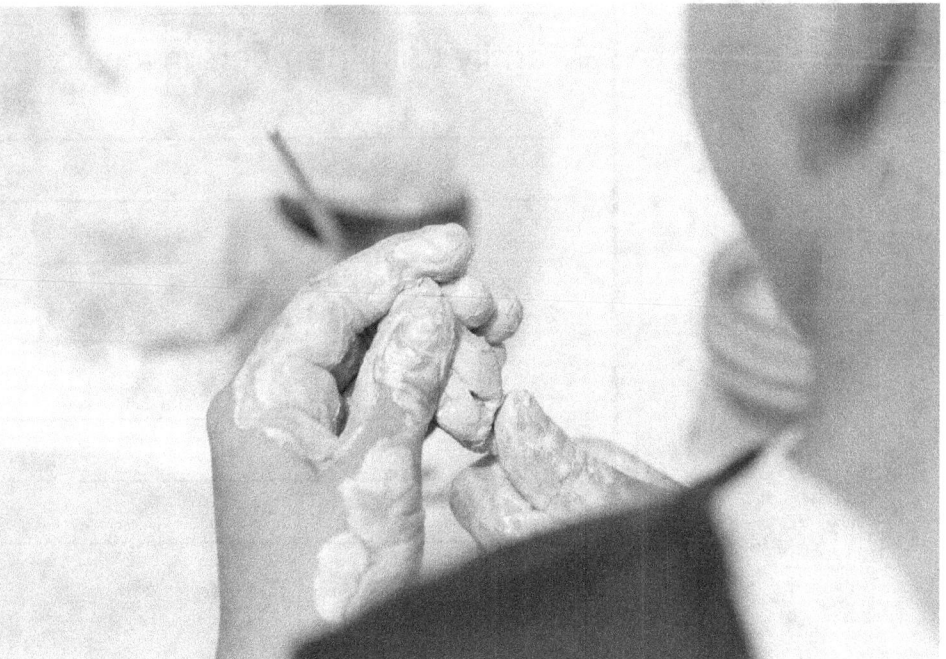

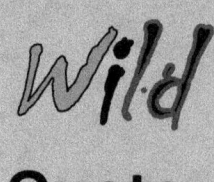

## Wild Quote

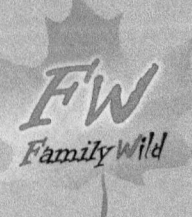

## Sculpting Project #1

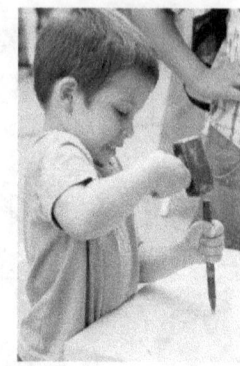

# Family Wild Log

Member Name_____

Date_____ Time _____

Member's Age _____ Location _____

Art Project _____

Art Medium Used _____

Wildlife or Nature Included

_____

_____

_____

Family Wild Members involved (names)

_____

_____

_____

Special Memories _____

_____

_____

_____

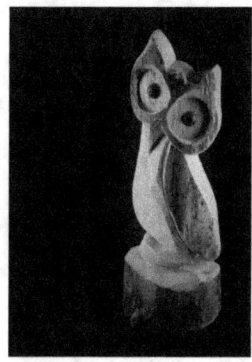

## Sculpting Project #2

# Family Wild Log

"Anybody with artistic ambitions is trying to reconnect with the way they saw things as a child."

**Tim Burton**
American Actor/ Director

Member Name_____

Date_____ Time _____

Member's Age _____ Location _____

Art Project _____

Art Medium Used _____

Wildlife or Nature Included

_____

_____

_____

Family Wild Members involved (names)

_____

_____

_____

Special Memories _____

_____

_____

_____

_____

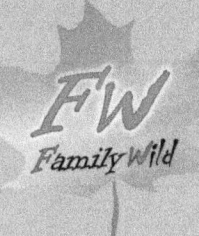

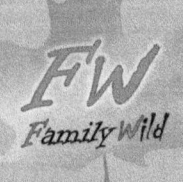
## Sculpting Project #3

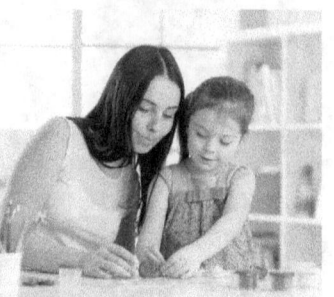

# Family Wild Log

Member Name_____

Date_____ Time _____

Member's Age _____ Location _____

Art Project _____

Art Medium Used _____

Wildlife or Nature Included

_____

_____

_____

Family Wild Members involved (names)

_____

_____

_____

Special Memories _____

_____

_____

_____

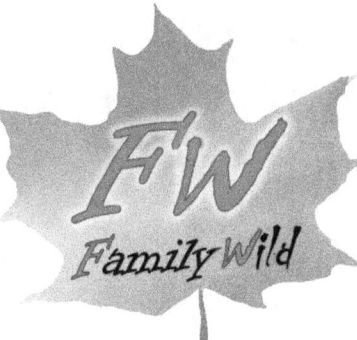

# Family Wild

Herby certifies that

_____

## Earned FamilyWild's

# Sculpting Slam

Date _____  Project _____

Date _____  Project _____

Date _____  Project _____

_____          *Michael Nunneley*

FamilyWild Local Chapter President          FamilyWild National President

# SLAM PICTURES

## Glue a couple pictures here

## to remember your SLAM!

You can keep the pictures in your book or put them
on the back of your certificate in a frame to
commemorate your art work!

**Below, take a few minutes to tell your story in your own words.**

Think of it as telling your grandchildren about your
art experience. It will be like sending a post card to
someone who will read it 50-100 years from now!

## My Slam Story

_____

_____

_____

_____

_____

_____

_____

# Videography Slam

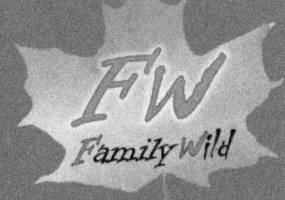

*FW*
*Family Wild*

"An artist

is an

explorer."

## Henri
## Matisse
French
Artist

I'm not sure that anything has grown as quickly as the outdoor videography world. Now, many hunters head to the woods with their video cameras or Go-Pros to document their hunts. The same goes for the fishing world as anglers capture their once-in-a-lifetime catches. Not to mention, countless plain old video enthusiast.

To earn this Slam, your budding videographers need to create, produce and edit three different projects including a YouTube Short, Blog Video Entry or a Facebook Video. They can also capture a hunting trip on video, a fishing trip on video, record an outdoor based construction or art project, or create a short story and/or educational video.

We encourage you all to try your hand on one side of the video camera or the other. As with many of our projects, the true value of this slam comes when your youngest members show these Wild videos to their grandchildren fifty years from now!

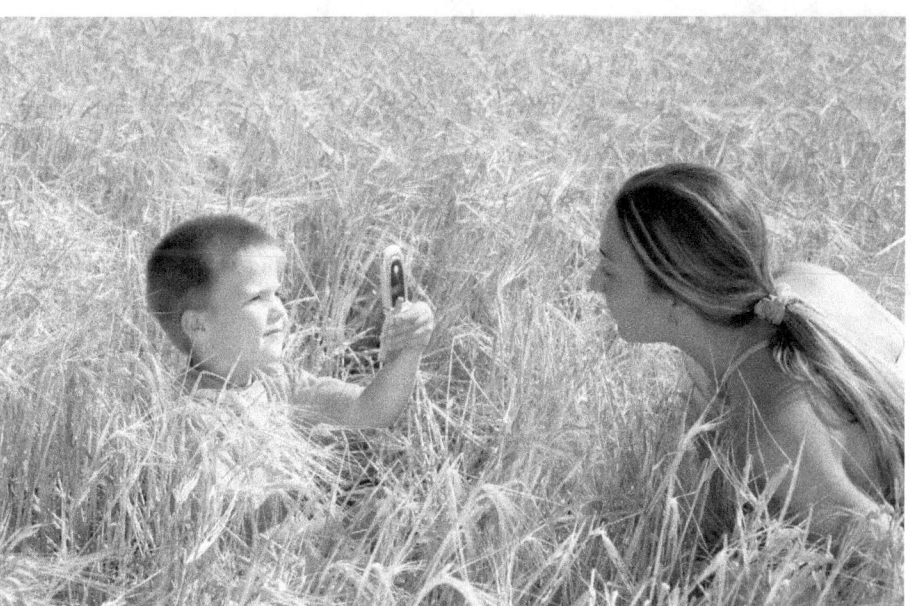

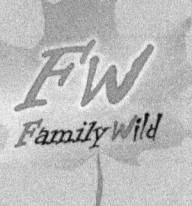

*FW*
*Family Wild*

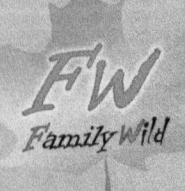
# Videography Project #1

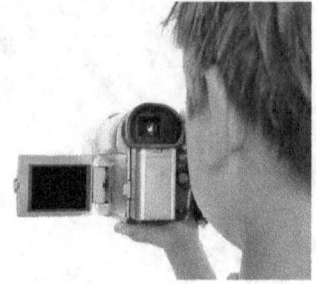

## Family Wild Log

Member Name _____

Date _____ Time _____

Member's Age _____ Location _____

Art Project _____

Art Medium Used _____

Wildlife or Nature Included

_____

_____

_____

Family Wild Members involved (names)

_____

_____

_____

Special Memories _____

_____

_____

_____

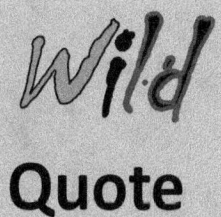
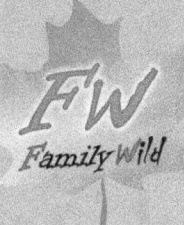
## Videography Project #2

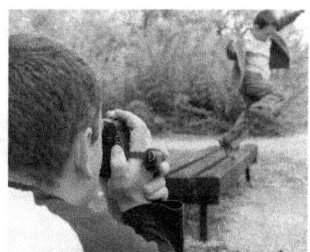

# Family Wild Log

Member Name _____

Date _____ Time _____

Member's Age _____ Location _____

Art Project _____

Art Medium Used _____

Wildlife or Nature Included

_____

_____

_____

Family Wild Members involved (names)

_____

_____

_____

Special Memories _____

_____

_____

_____

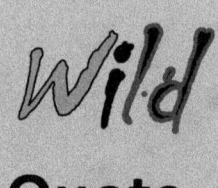

## Quote

"To live life, we must lose our fear of being wrong."

**Joseph Chilton Pearce** American Author

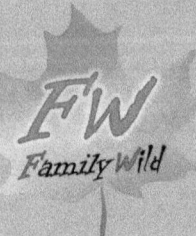
Family Wild

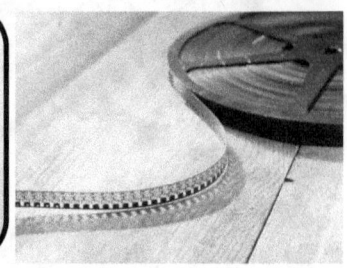

# Videography Project #3

## Family Wild Log

Member Name_____

Date_____ Time _____

Member's Age _____ Location _____

Art Project _____

Art Medium Used _____

Wildlife or Nature Included

_____

_____

_____

Family Wild Members involved (names)

_____

_____

_____

Special Memories _____

_____

_____

_____

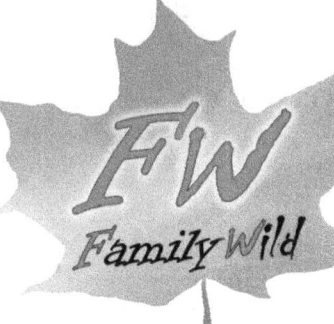

# Family Wild

*Herby certifies that*

_____

## *Earned Family Wild's*

# Videography Slam

Date _____ Project _____

Date _____ Project _____

Date _____ Project _____

_____         *Michael Nunneley*

*Family Wild Local Chapter President*      *Family Wild National President*

# SLAM PICTURES

## Glue a couple pictures here

## to remember your SLAM!

You can keep the pictures in your book or put them
on the back of your certificate in a frame to
commemorate your art work!

**Below, take a few minutes to tell your story in your own words.**

Think of it as telling your grandchildren about your
art experience. It will be like sending a post card to
someone who will read it 50-100 years from now!

# My Slam Story

_____

_____

_____

_____

_____

_____

_____

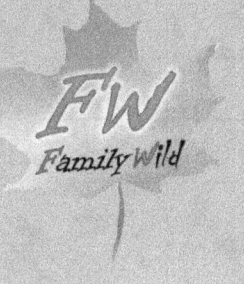
# Textile Arts Slam

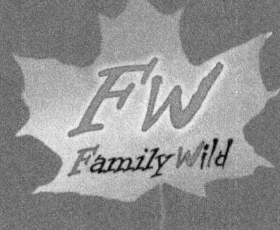

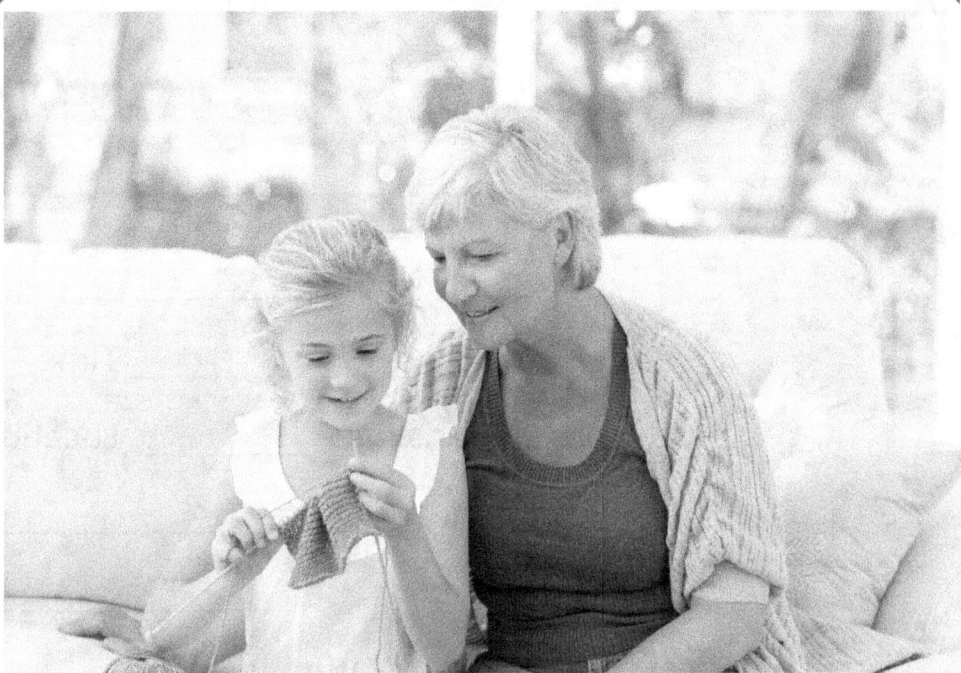

Not all wildlife arts happen outside. The earliest cavemen and women, as well as early American Pioneers, had to craft a variety of things for sheer survival. Truth be told, we've both (yes M.W. too) even made a hunting hat or two for our children and family.

Your members will need to try to make a total of three textile project including blankets, quilts, clothing, placemats, pillows or warm hunting apparel. Remember, the theme for these must be wildlife or the outdoors to qualify for the Slam.

You may have to consult YouTube or check at the local arts and crafts store, library, or museum for someone to help you learn these Wild time-honored arts.

## Wild
### Quote

"Creativity is more than just being different. Anybody can plan weird; that's easy. What's hard is to be as simple as Bach. Making the simple, awesomely simple, that's creativity."

## Charles Mingus
American Bassist

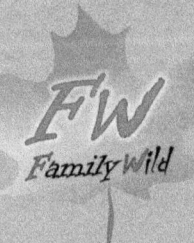

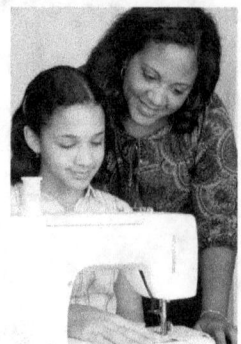

## Textile Project #1

# Family Wild Log

Member Name_____

Date_____ Time _____

Member's Age _____ Location _____

Art Project _____

Art Medium Used _____

Wildlife or Nature Included

_____

_____

_____

Family Wild Members involved (names)

_____

_____

_____

Special Memories _____

_____

_____

_____

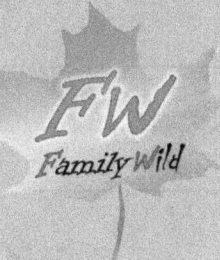

## Textile Project #2

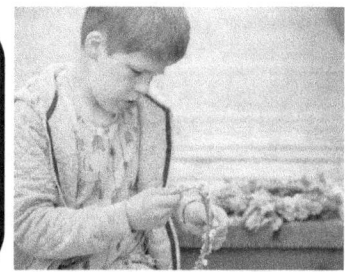

# Family Wild Log

Member Name_____

Date_____ Time _____

Member's Age _____ Location _____

Art Project _____

Art Medium Used _____

Wildlife or Nature Included

_____

_____

_____

Family Wild Members involved (names)

_____

_____

_____

Special Memories _____

_____

_____

_____

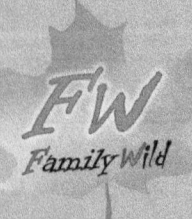

## Textile Project #3

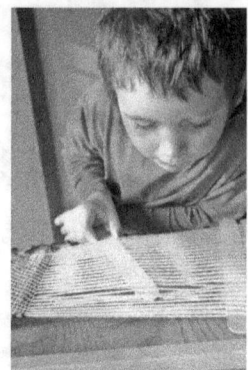

# Family Wild Log

Member Name_____

Date_____ Time _____

Member's Age _____ Location _____

Art Project _____

Art Medium Used _____

Wildlife or Nature Included

_____

_____

_____

Family Wild Members involved (names)

_____

_____

_____

Special Memories _____

_____

_____

_____

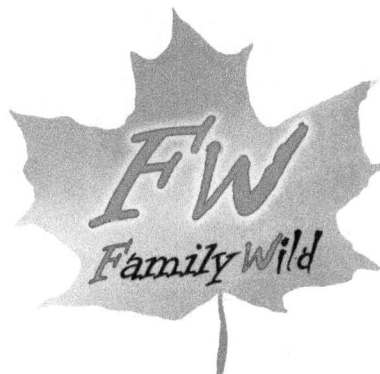

# *Family Wild*

*Herby certifies that*

_____

## *Earned Family Wild's*

# Textile Slam

| | |
|---|---|
| **Date** _____ | **Project** _____ |
| **Date** _____ | **Project** _____ |
| **Date** _____ | **Project** _____ |
| _____ | *Michael Nunneley* |
| *Family Wild Local Chapter President* | *Family Wild National President* |

# SLAM PICTURES

## Glue a couple pictures here

## to remember your SLAM!

You can keep the pictures in your book or put them
on the back of your certificate in a frame to
commemorate your art work!

**Below, take a few minutes to tell your story in your own words.**

Think of it as telling your grandchildren about your
art experience. It will be like sending a post card to
someone who will read it 50-100 years from now!

# My Slam Story

_____

_____

_____

_____

_____

_____

_____

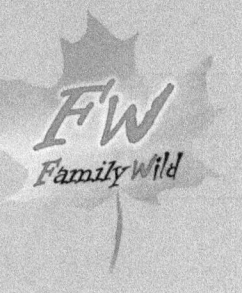
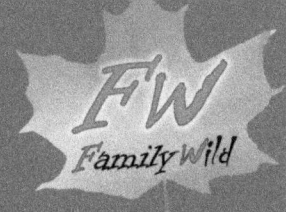

# Trail Cam Slam

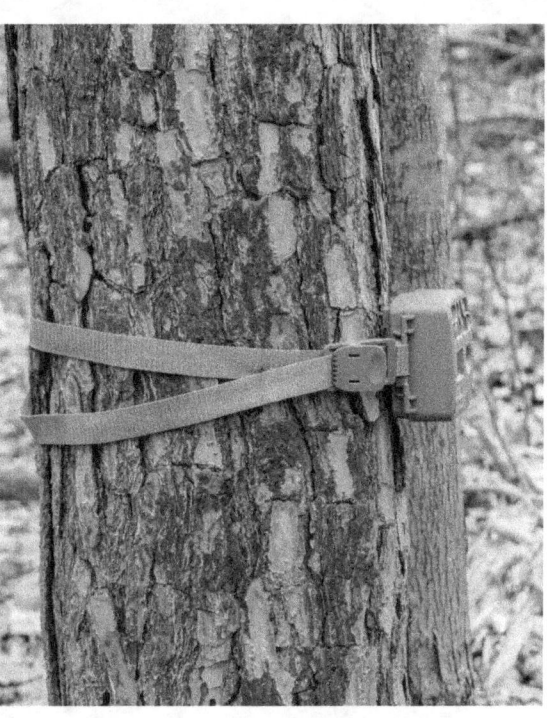

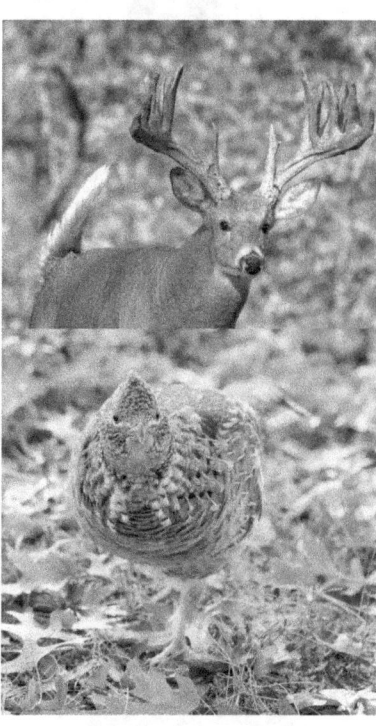

One of our favorite things to do year round on our property is check the trail cams. We both enjoy the walk as we pull cards and then scamper back to the computer to see what we "captured." We keep waiting to see Bigfoot or a Dogman of Michigan but no luck just yet.

For this slam you need to grab at least 7 of the following animal categories to qualify: Small Game, Varmint, Predator, Deer, Big Game, Game Bird, Wild Bird, Trapper, and/or Waterfowl.

As a bonus, if you do capture Bigfoot, a Werewolf, a Dogman of Michigan or anything else you might see Sam & Dean chase on *Supernatural*, you can use that in place of one of your 7 animals. You think we're kidding? We're not. Include a Wild *Supernatural* Trail Cam image as part of this Slam! Use your imagination and if you get a great image, send it to our website, we'd love to see it!

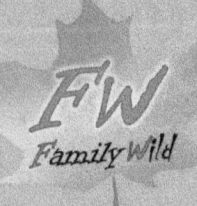
## Trail Cam Project #1

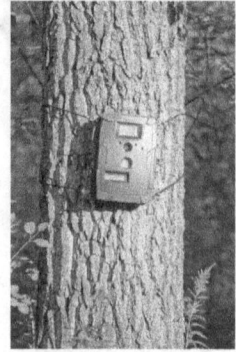

# Family Wild Log

Member Name_____

Date_____ Time _____

Member's Age _____ Location _____

Art Project _____

Art Medium Used _____

Wildlife or Nature Included

_____

_____

_____

Family Wild Members involved (names)

_____

_____

_____

Special Memories _____

_____

_____

_____

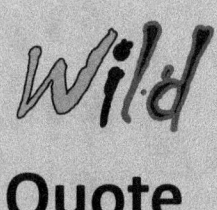
**Trail Cam Project #2**

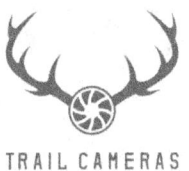

TRAIL CAMERAS

## Family Wild Log

"Creative isn't the way I think, it's the way I like to live."

**Paul Sandip** Producer

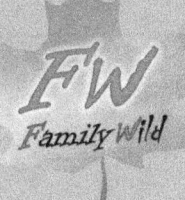

Member Name_____

Date_____ Time _____

Member's Age _____ Location _____

Art Project _____

Art Medium Used _____

Wildlife or Nature Included

_____

_____

_____

Family Wild Members involved (names)

_____

_____

_____

Special Memories _____

_____

_____

_____

_____

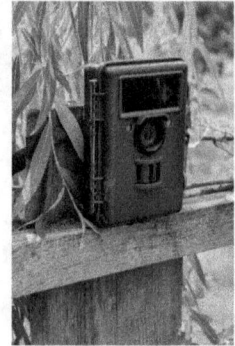

## Trail Cam Project #3

"Creativity is inventing, experimenting, growing, taking risks, breaking rules, making mistakes, and having fun."

**Mary Lou Cook**
Peace Activist

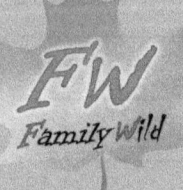

FW
Family Wild

# Family Wild Log

Member Name_____

Date_____ Time _____

Member's Age _____ Location _____

Art Project _____

Art Medium Used _____

Wildlife or Nature Included

_____

_____

_____

Family Wild Members involved (names)

_____

_____

_____

Special Memories _____

_____

_____

_____

_____

# Construction Slam

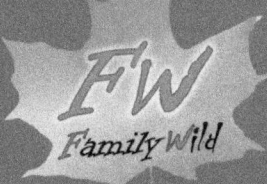

## Wild Quote

"The artist is not a special kind of person; rather, each person is a special kind of artist."

**Ananda Coomara-swamy**
Philosopher

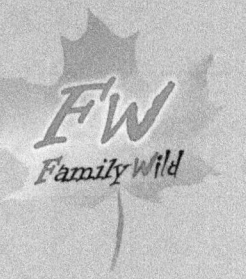

From the first lean-to to the huge hunting lodges of today, we've been constructing things in the woods and along lakes for millennia. Here's your chance to get out the hammer, nails, and power tools to earn your Construction Slam.

You need to construct three projects to earn this one at three different levels. One project needs to be small - like building a bird house. A second project needs to be a big project - like building a fish shelter or deer blind. The third project needs to improve our outdoors - like repairing and painting a park sign.

As with all of our art projects, you are only limited by your imagination. If you video or photograph your efforts you can work towards earning additional slams. Have fun with this and enjoy teaching your younger members how to safely build things big and small. If you're

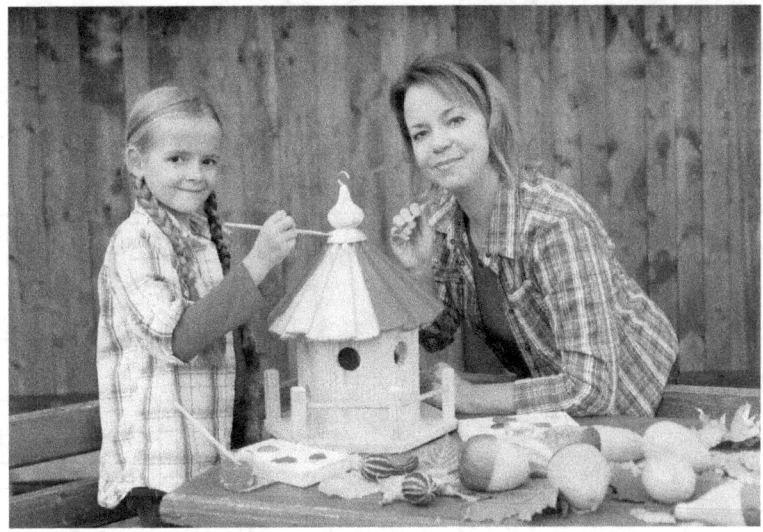

not into building yourself, do what we did and check out YouTube for tips. I always gravitate towards our Canadian friends as they seem to be the most hands-on and creative folks, filled with Wild construction ideas!

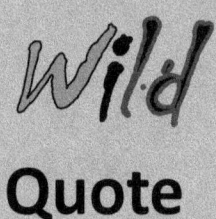
## Construction Project #1

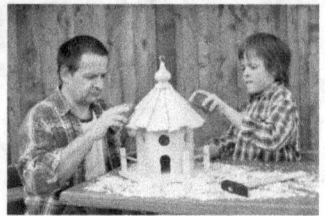

"Every

artist was

first an

amateur."

**Ralph
Waldo
Emerson**
American
Poet

# Family Wild Log

Member Name_____

Date_____ Time _____

Member's Age _____ Location _____

Art Project _____

Art Medium Used _____

Wildlife or Nature Included

_____

_____

_____

Family Wild Members involved (names)

_____

_____

_____

Special Memories _____

_____

_____

_____

_____

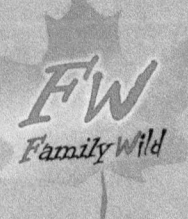

**FW**
*Family Wild*

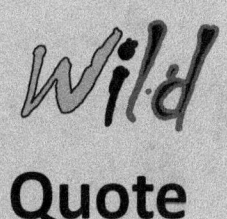

## Wild
**Quote**

"Art

takes

nature

as its

model."

**Aristotle**
Greek
Philosopher

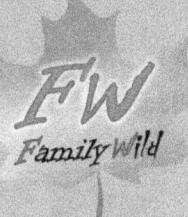
*FW*
*Family Wild*

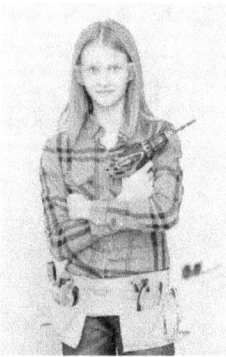

## Construction Project #2

# Family Wild Log

Member Name_____

Date_____ Time _____

Member's Age _____ Location _____

Art Project _____

Art Medium Used _____

Wildlife or Nature Included

_____

_____

_____

Family Wild Members involved (names)

_____

_____

_____

Special Memories _____

_____

_____

_____

_____

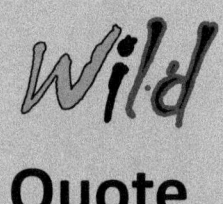

**Quote**

"You can't use up creativity. The more you use the more you have."

**Maya Angelou**
American Poet

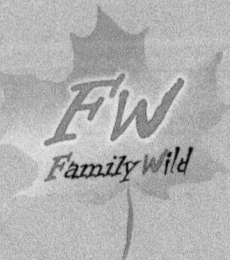

## Construction Project #3

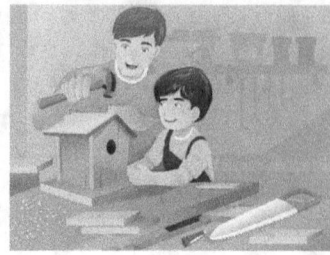

# Family Wild Log

Member Name_____

Date_____ Time _____

Member's Age _____ Location _____

Art Project _____

Art Medium Used _____

Wildlife or Nature Included

_____

_____

_____

Family Wild Members involved (names)

_____

_____

_____

Special Memories _____

_____

_____

_____

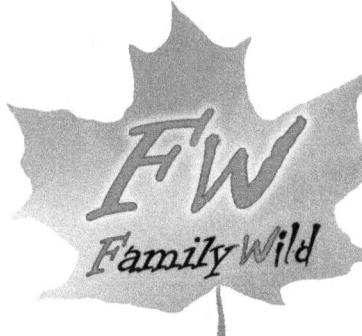

# Family Wild

*Herby certifies that*

_____

*Earned FamilyWild's*

# Construction Slam

| | |
|---|---|
| **Date** _____ | **Project** _____ |
| **Date** _____ | **Project** _____ |
| **Date** _____ | **Project** _____ |

_____          *Michael Nunneley*

*FamilyWild Local Chapter President*          *FamilyWild National President*

# SLAM PICTURES

## Glue a couple pictures here

## to remember your SLAM!

You can keep the pictures in your book or put them
on the back of your certificate in a frame to
commemorate your art work!

**Below, take a few minutes to tell your story in your own words.**

Think of it as telling your grandchildren about your
art experience. It will be like sending a post card to
someone who will read it 50-100 years from now!

## My Slam Story

_____

_____

_____

_____

_____

_____

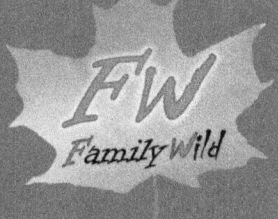

# Plant Pressing Slam

## Wild Quote

"If a child is to keep alive his inborn sense of wonder, he needs the companion-ship of at least one adult who can share it, rediscovering with him the joy, excitement and mystery of the world we live in."

**Rachel Carson**
Marine Biologist

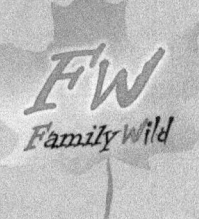

Plant and flower pressing naturally preserves plant specimens. The dried flowers and leaves can be catalogued and identified for future reference and as collectibles. As you see below, you can also press flowers to be used for creative purposes like greeting cards, scrapbooks and floral arrangements. You can also give a 3-D effect to paintings, flower pots, and decoupage glue projects.

The beauty of flower and plant pressing really comes from getting to know your land and the areas around your home. Be sure to invest in a flower and plant guide and identify it before you pick! Not only will this keep you from carefully drying poison ivy (a very itchy mistake), it will also help you be compliant with local wildflower protection laws.

For instance, corn flowers are everywhere in our field in the summer and are wonderful in the press. But it's illegal to pick and press trillium, a lovely three-petaled white spring flower. Your identification process will also help you find herbs and edible plants that will be useful as you learn to "wildcraft" and enjoy some of nature's bounty on your table or as part of your medicine cabinet.

Members of all ages can enjoy hours of collecting leaves and flowers, transforming them into endless art projects and learning about the plant life in your part of the world. Let your imagination run WILD as you earn your Pressing Slam.

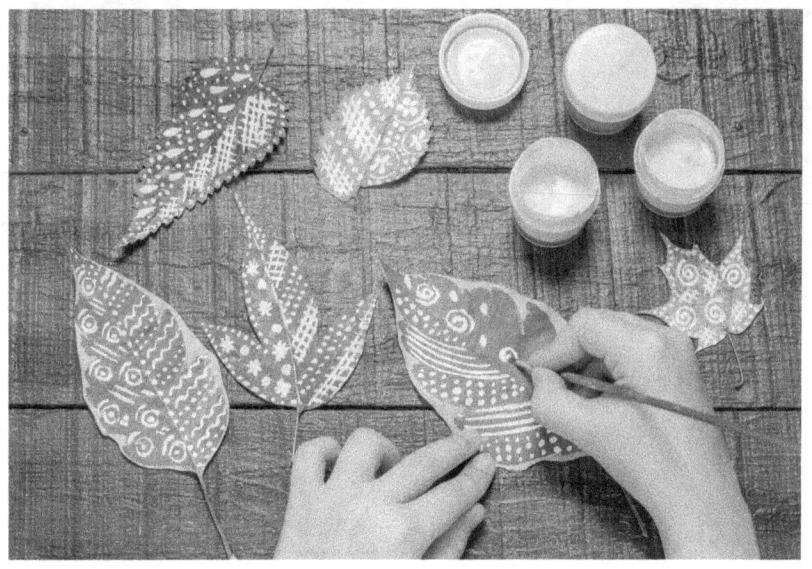

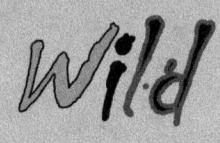

# Wild
## Quote

"The world is but a canvas to the imagina-tion."

**Henry David Thoreau** American Poet

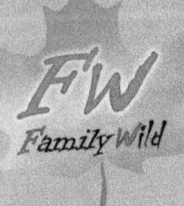

FW
Family Wild

## Plant Pressing Slam Project #1

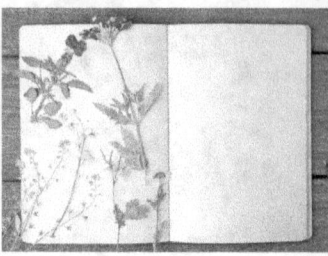

# Family Wild Log

Member Name_____

Date_____ Time _____

Member's Age _____ Location _____

Art Project _____

Art Medium Used _____

Wildlife or Nature Included

_____

_____

_____

Family Wild Members involved (names)

_____

_____

_____

Special Memories _____

_____

_____

_____

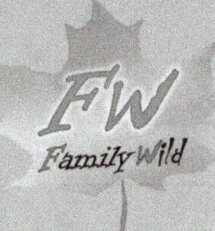
# Plant Pressing Slam Project #2

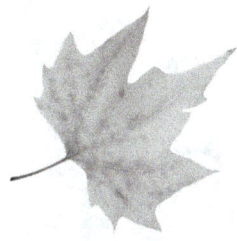

## Family Wild Log

Member Name _____

Date _____ Time _____

Member's Age _____ Location _____

Art Project _____

Art Medium Used _____

Wildlife or Nature Included

_____

_____

_____

Family Wild Members involved (names)

_____

_____

_____

Special Memories _____

_____

_____

_____

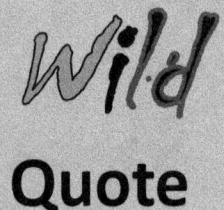
**Plant Pressing Slam Project #3**

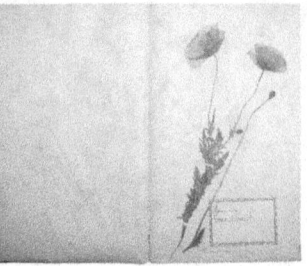

"Imagina-

tion is more

important

than

knowledge."

**Albert Einstein** German- American Physicist

# *Family Wild Log*

Member Name_____

Date_____ Time _____

Member's Age _____ Location _____

Art Project _____

Art Medium Used _____

Wildlife or Nature Included

_____

_____

_____

Family Wild Members involved (names)

_____

_____

_____

Special Memories _____

_____

_____

_____

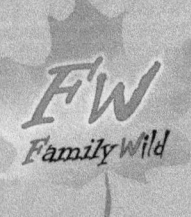

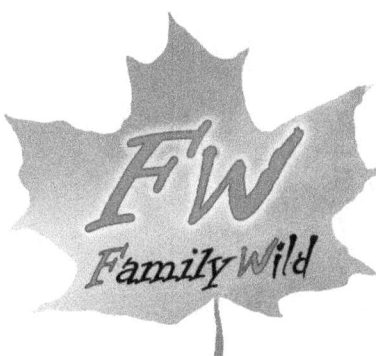

# Family Wild

*Herby certifies that*

_____

*Earned Family Wild's*

# Plant Pressing Slam

**Date** _____ **Project** _____

**Place** _____

**Working with** _____

_____        *Michael Nunneley*

*Family Wild Local Chapter President*        *Family Wild National President*

# SLAM PICTURES

## Glue a couple pictures here

## to remember your SLAM!

You can keep the pictures in your book or put them
on the back of your certificate in a frame to
commemorate your art work!

**Below, take a few minutes to tell your story in your own words.**

Think of it as telling your grandchildren about your
art experience. It will be like sending a post card to
someone who will read it 50-100 years from now!

# My Slam Story

_____

_____

_____

_____

_____

_____

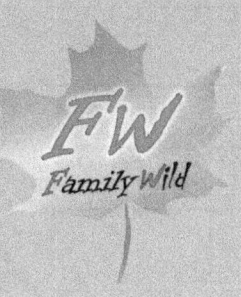
# Scrapbook/ Journal Slam

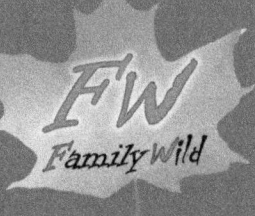

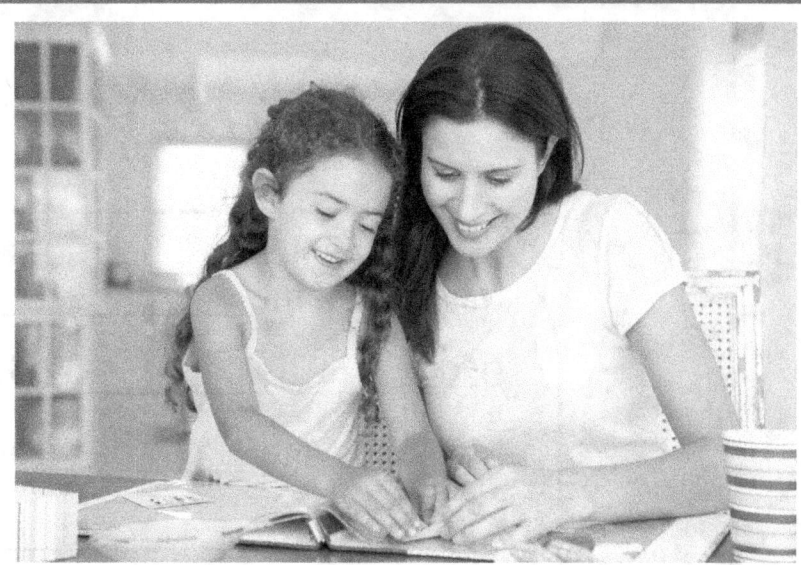

I don't know about you, but I LOVE looking at old scrapbooks - seeing people when they were young or much younger; trying to figure out how grandpa had so much hair back then; how grandma looked before she could take her teeth out at night.

Never underestimate the joy of a journal full of a young child's drawings. Make a big deal out of decorating a simple Dollar Store or Goodwill binder or notebook, and encourage your kids to capture the wild in crayon, pencil or even water colors. If you look at the journals I (Kim) have kept since sixth grade, they are full of sketches, doodles, garden layouts, and more. It's perfectly OK to combine the journal and scrapbook experience with other slams - so a drawing in your journal can also qualify for a part of the drawing slam, or adding a print picture taken during a trip to the lake works in the photography slam.

To be able to enjoy those pictures and moments, someone had to craft a scrapbook. To qualify for this slam, the Family Wild member must create and keep a Scrapbook or a Journal for at least three months, but we recommend keeping it going much longer!

As a photographer, I (Mike) treasure the value of an image. When you place it in a scrapbook, you only magnify the story for your family. Add a journal or journal entry and you'll send postcards to the future for your family to enjoy for generations. That's WILD!

# Scrapbook/Journal Project #1

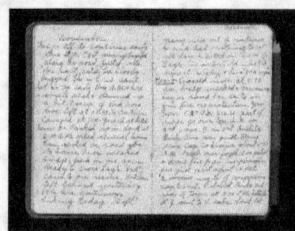

## Family Wild Log

Member Name _____

Date _____ Time _____

Member's Age _____ Location _____

Art Project _____

Art Medium Used _____

Wildlife or Nature Included

_____

_____

_____

Family Wild Members involved (names)

_____

_____

_____

Special Memories _____

_____

_____

_____

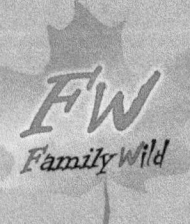

FW
Family Wild

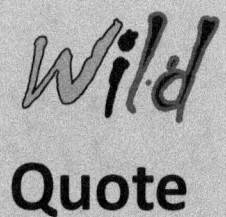

# Wild
## Quote

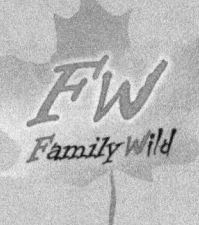

**FW**
*Family Wild*

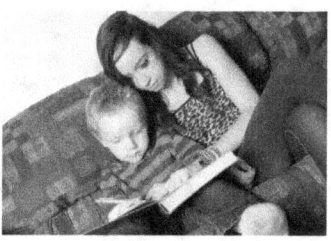

## Scrapbook/Journal Project #2

# Family Wild Log

Member Name_____

Date_____ Time _____

Member's Age _____ Location _____

Art Project _____

Art Medium Used _____

Wildlife or Nature Included

_____

_____

_____

Family Wild Members involved (names)

_____

_____

_____

Special Memories _____

_____

_____

_____

_____

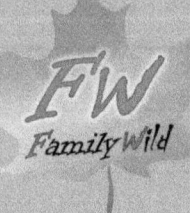

# Scrapbook/Journal Project #3

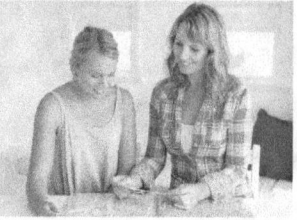

## Family Wild Log

Member Name_____

Date_____ Time _____

Member's Age _____ Location _____

Art Project _____

Art Medium Used _____

Wildlife or Nature Included

_____

_____

_____

Family Wild Members involved (names)

_____

_____

_____

Special Memories _____

_____

_____

_____

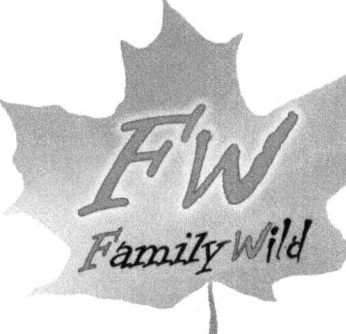

# *Family Wild*

*Herby certifies that*

_____

*Earned FamilyWild's*

# Scrapbook/Journal Slam

| | |
|---|---|
| **Date** _____ | **Project** _____ |
| **Date** _____ | **Project** _____ |
| **Date** _____ | **Project** _____ |

_____

*FamilyWild Local Chapter President*

*Michael Nunneley*

*FamilyWild National President*

# SLAM PICTURES

## Glue a couple pictures here

## to remember your SLAM!

You can keep the pictures in your book or put them
on the back of your certificate in a frame to
commemorate your art work!

**Below, take a few minutes to tell your story in your own words.**

Think of it as telling your grandchildren about your
art experience. It will be like sending a post card to
someone who will read it 50-100 years from now!

# My Slam Story

_____

_____

_____

_____

_____

_____

# Taxidermy Slam

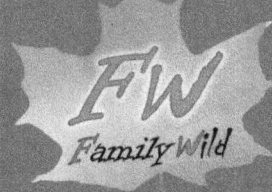

"I was just different. When the other kids gravitated to football or basketball, I went fishing and skating. I was into trapping animals, pheasants and squirrels. Not only was I a trapper, I was a taxidermist."

**Gene Pitney**
American Singer

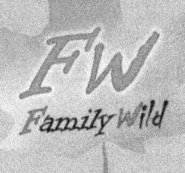

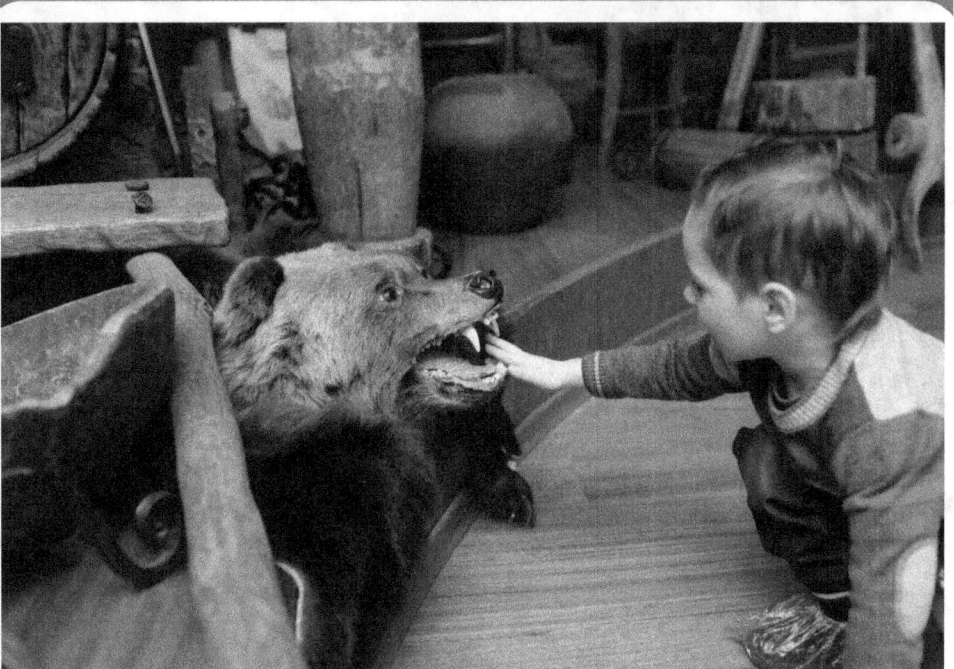

We recently went to a wildlife show in Grand Rapids, MI. There we encountered multiple species mounted on display by novice to world class taxidermists. The days of "stuffing" a head or fish on the wall have given way to delicate artistic expression.

To earn this slam you must either process three hides (tanning) or craft three mounts of either fish, reptiles or mammals. You can also produce a combination of tanning projects and mounts to earn this Slam.

Today's masters all started the same way, as a new taxidermist learning or apprenticing the craft. One of my youth hockey players earned spending money as a novice taxidermist. He got paid very well for learning his craft as folks who couldn't afford a $500 to $1000 mount were happy to pay him a couple hundred dollars.

Seek out local experts, classes, websites, YouTube, books or videos to help guide you into a Wild lifetime of preserving animals.

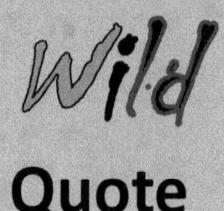
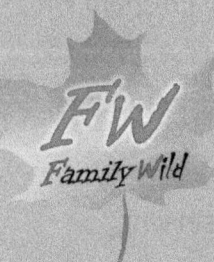
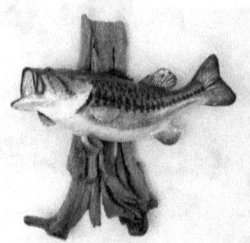

## Taxidermy/Tanning Project #1

# Family Wild Log

Member Name_____

Date_____ Time _____

Member's Age _____ Location _____

Art Project _____

Art Medium Used _____

Wildlife or Nature Included

_____

_____

_____

Family Wild Members involved (names)

_____

_____

_____

Special Memories _____

_____

_____

_____

_____

# Wild Quote

"Color provokes a psychic vibration. Color hides a power still unknown but real, which acts on every part of the human body."

**Wassily Kandinsky** Russian Painter

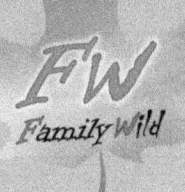

## Taxidermy/Tanning Project #2

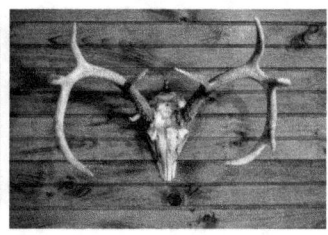

# Family Wild Log

Member Name_____

Date_____ Time _____

Member's Age _____ Location _____

Art Project _____

Art Medium Used _____

Wildlife or Nature Included

_____

_____

_____

Family Wild Members involved (names)

_____

_____

_____

Special Memories _____

_____

_____

_____

"Whether you succeed or not is irrelevant, there is no such thing. Making your unknown known is the important thing—and keeping the unknown always beyond you."

**Georgia O'Keefe** American Artist

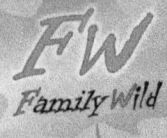

## Taxidermy/Tanning Project #3

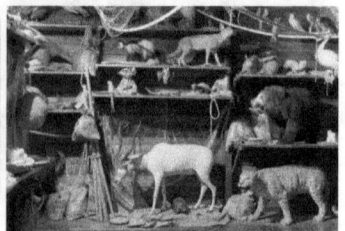

# Family Wild Log

Member Name _____

Date _____ Time _____

Member's Age _____ Location _____

Art Project _____

Art Medium Used _____

Wildlife or Nature Included

_____

_____

_____

Family Wild Members involved (names)

_____

_____

_____

Special Memories _____

_____

_____

_____

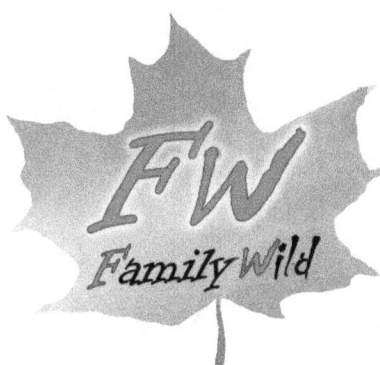

# Family Wild

*Herby certifies that*

_____

*Earned Family Wild's*

# Taxidermy/Tanning Slam

Date _____ Project _____

Place _____

Working with _____

_____     *Michael Nunneley*

*FamilyWild Local Chapter President*     *FamilyWild National President*

# SLAM PICTURES

## *Glue a couple pictures here*

## *to remember your SLAM!*

You can keep the pictures in your book or put them
on the back of your certificate in a frame to
commemorate your art work!

**Below, take a few minutes to tell your story in your own words.**

Think of it as telling your grandchildren about your
art experience. It will be like sending a post card to
someone who will read it 50-100 years from now!

# My Slam Story

_____

_____

_____

_____

_____

_____

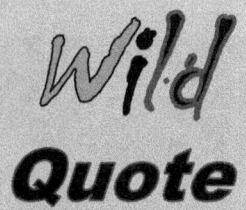
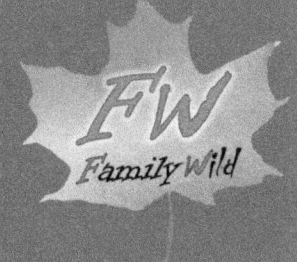

# Music Slam

"**Music is**

**the art of**

**thinking**

**with**

**sounds.**"

**Julies
Combarieu**
French
Music
Scholar

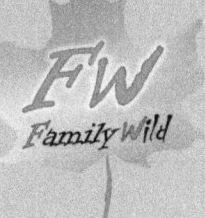

From the day a cave dweller took a rock and beat it on another rock, we've made music. You may not think of music as an outdoor activity, but we've decided to make it one!

To earn this slam, you have to truly get creative. You have to make music in three different ways. You can create instruments from nature (wood, rocks, long grass, water), you can make music with man-made instruments using outdoor noises as accompaniment (the wind, water, spring peeper frogs, crickets), you can write a song featuring the outdoors, animals, birds or fish, you can record and identify outdoor sounds (birds, animals, outdoor noises) or you might do Mp3 Shares with nature themes.

We'll even let you qualify a Family Wild Karaoke, but you have to go to the utensil drawer and get out soup ladle "microphones" and make a video or take pictures to document the experience.

At one of the camps I joined years ago, the best night of Hunting Season was Soup Ladle Karaoke Night to an old radio! We still talk about those Wild times!

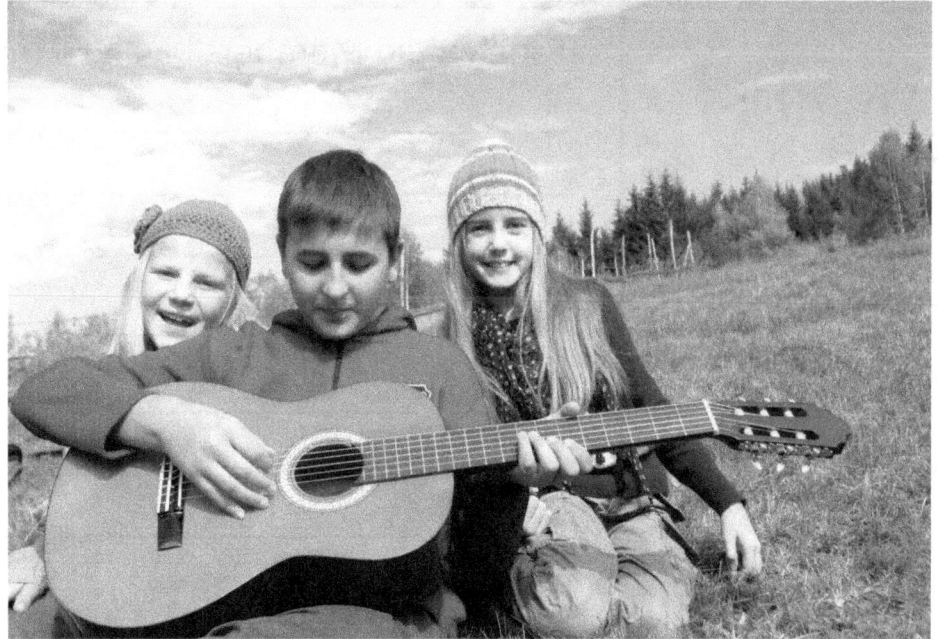

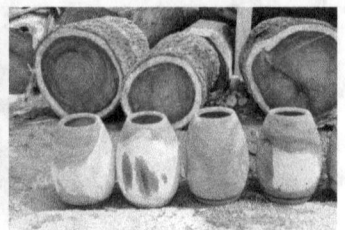

## Music Slam
## Project #1

"Music is your own experience, your own thoughts, your wisdom. If you don't live it, it won't come out of your horn. They teach you there's a boundary line to music. But, man, there's no boundary line to art."

## Charles Parker

American Saxophonist

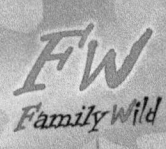

# Family Wild Log

Member Name_____

Date_____ Time _____

Member's Age _____ Location _____

Art Project _____

Art Medium Used _____

Wildlife or Nature Included

_____

_____

_____

Family Wild Members involved (names)

_____

_____

_____

Special Memories _____

_____

_____

_____

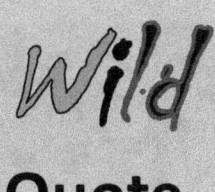
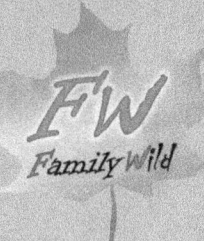
## Music Slam
## Project #2

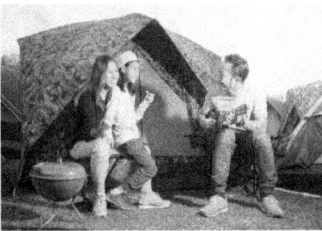

# Family Wild Log

Member Name_____

Date_____ Time _____

Member's Age _____ Location _____

Art Project _____

Art Medium Used _____

Wildlife or Nature Included

_____

_____

_____

Family Wild Members involved (names)

_____

_____

_____

Special Memories _____

_____

_____

_____

_____

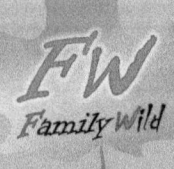

# Music Slam Project #3

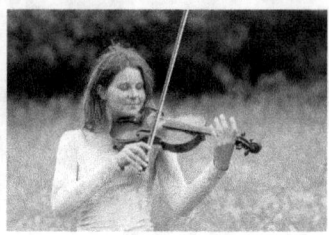

## Family Wild Log

Member Name_____

Date_____ Time _____

Member's Age _____ Location _____

Art Project _____

Art Medium Used _____

Wildlife or Nature Included

_____

_____

_____

Family Wild Members involved (names)

_____

_____

_____

Special Memories _____

_____

_____

_____

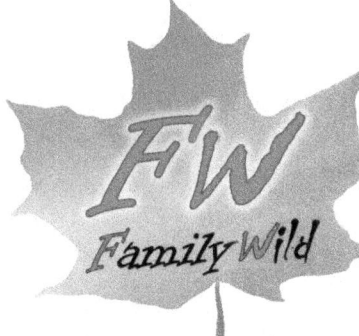

# Family Wild

*Herby certifies that*

_____

*Earned FamilyWild's*

# Music Slam

Date _____    Project_____

Date _____    Project_____

Date _____    Project_____

_____          *Michael Nunneley*

*FamilyWild Local Chapter President*          *FamilyWild National President*

# SLAM PICTURES

## Glue a couple pictures here

## to remember your SLAM!

You can keep the pictures in your book or put them
on the back of your certificate in a frame to
commemorate your art work!

**Below, take a few minutes to tell your story in your own words.**

Think of it as telling your grandchildren about your
art experience. It will be like sending a post card to
someone who will read it 50-100 years from now!

## My Slam Story

_____

_____

_____

_____

_____

_____

_____

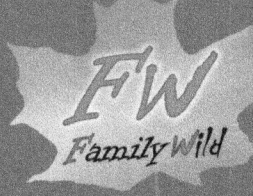

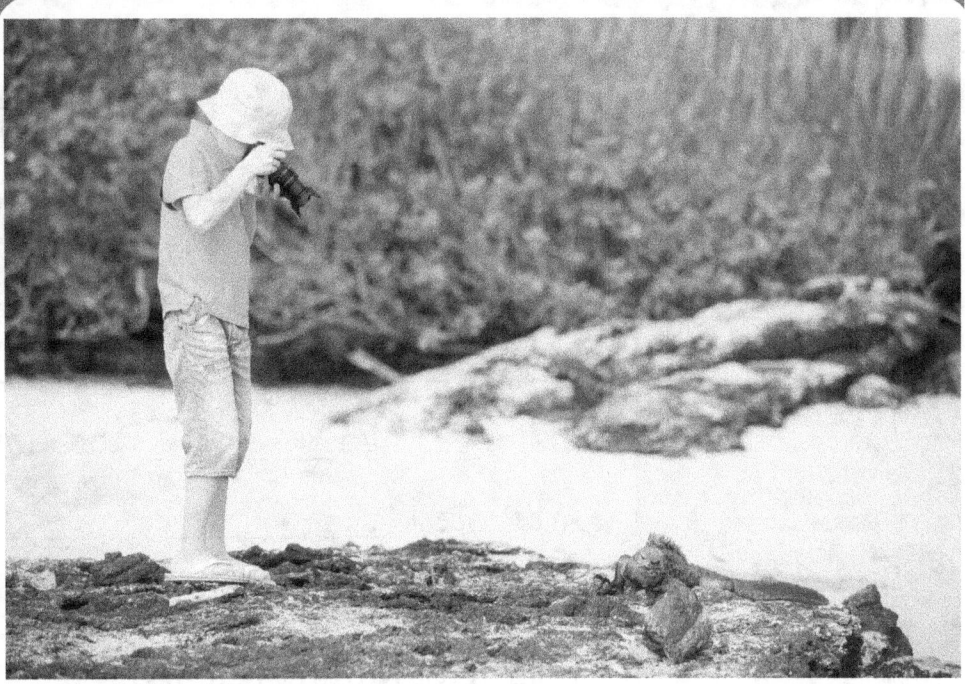

Of all the Art Slams, this one comes from my heart! As a professional photographer, there was nothing more satisfying than capturing a once-in-a-lifetime moment on film (we used this thing called film years ago). The anticipation of waiting for an hour or a couple days (we used to have to take our "film" to someone to develop it and make prints of it) was nerve-wracking. The only difference between this and hunting or fishing is you don't have to clean what you catch!

To earn my *favorite* Art Slam, you need to click at least 10 different photos from a hunting or fishing trip. You can record any of your Hunting, Fishing or Art Slam moments in a picture. You can also photographically hunt down one animal from each of the following Small Game, Varmint, Predator, Deer, Big Game, Game Bird, Wild Bird, Trapper, and/or Waterfowl as part of your ten.

As with trail cams, if you do capture Bigfoot, a Werewolf, a Dogman of Michigan, you can use that in place of one of your ten photo projects. You think we're kidding? Have fun creating it! Include a Wild Supernatural Trail Cam "image" as part of this Slam.

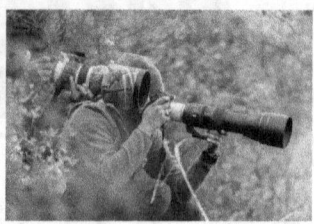

# Photography Slam Photo #1

*"You don't make a photograph just with a camera. You bring to the act of photography all the pictures you've seen, the books you have read, the music you have heard, the people you have loved."*

**Ansel Adams**
American Photographer

## Family Wild Log

Member Name_____

Date_____ Time _____

Member's Age _____ Location _____

Art Project _____

Art Medium Used _____

Wildlife or Nature Included

_____

_____

_____

Family Wild Members involved (names)

_____

_____

_____

Special Memories _____

_____

_____

_____

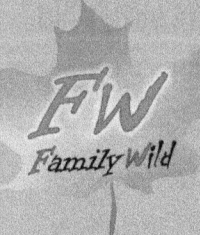

FW
*Family Wild*

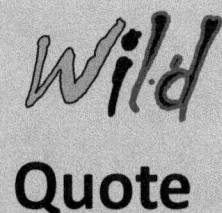

## Wild

### Quote

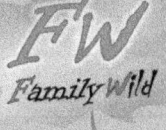

# Photography Slam Photo #2

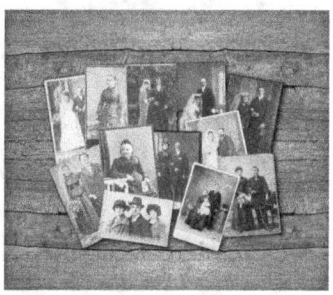

# Family Wild Log

Member Name_____

Date_____ Time _____

Member's Age _____ Location _____

Art Project _____

Art Medium Used _____

Wildlife or Nature Included

_____

_____

_____

Family Wild Members involved (names)

_____

_____

_____

Special Memories _____

_____

_____

_____

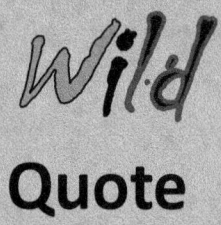

# Photography
# Slam Photo #3

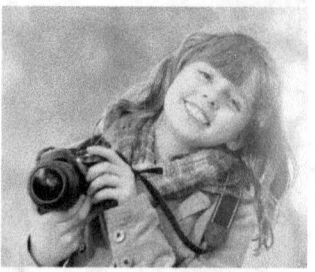

*"You don't*

*take a*

*photograph,*

*you make it."*

## Ansel
## Adams
### American
### Photographer

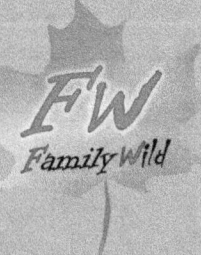

## *Family Wild Log*

Member Name_____

Date_____ Time _____

Member's Age _____ Location _____

Art Project _____

Art Medium Used _____

Wildlife or Nature Included

_____

_____

_____

Family Wild Members involved (names)

_____

_____

_____

Special Memories _____

_____

_____

_____

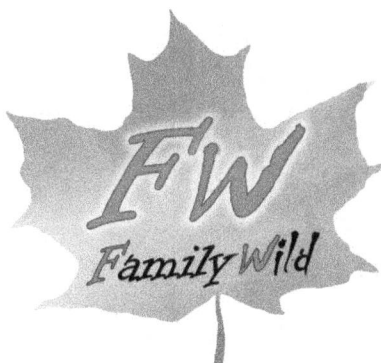

# Family Wild

*Herby certifies that*

_____

*Earned Family Wild's*

# Photography Slam

| | |
|---|---|
| **Date** _____ | **Project** _____ |
| **Date** _____ | **Project** _____ |
| **Date** _____ | **Project** _____ |

_____            *Michael Nunneley*

*Family Wild Local Chapter President*            *Family Wild National President*

# SLAM PICTURES

## Glue a couple pictures here

## to remember your SLAM!

You can keep the pictures in your book or put them
on the back of your certificate in a frame to
commemorate your art work!

**Below, take a few minutes to tell your story in your own words.**

Think of it as telling your grandchildren about your
art experience. It will be like sending a post card to
someone who will read it 50-100 years from now!

# My Slam Story

_____

_____

_____

_____

_____

_____

_____

# Recipes & Food Slam

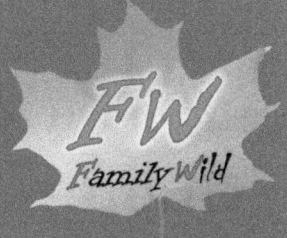

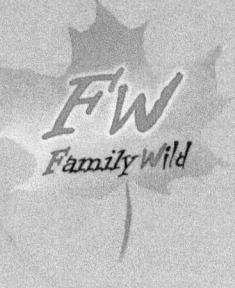
As long as someone has hunted and fished, there's been someone cooking what they captured and caught. Every camp and fishing cabin has those mouthwatering recipes that have come from trying "this" and adding "that!"

To earn this Slam, you can cook from a recipe taught to you by an adult Family Wild member and dish it out to the club. You can try cooking one of the recipes from your *Family Wild Hunting Camp Cookbook* or *Family Wild Fishing for a Recipe Book*. You can also make your own home-made tea, dehydrate your own wild game, can, freeze or freeze dry wild game, fruits or vegetables. We recommend you do this as a club or, at the very least, help out your younger members.

Shooting and catching are only part of the outdoor experience. Gutting or cleaning your kill or catch is part of the process. At the end of the processing is cooking, followed by my personal favorite part - WILD EATING!!!

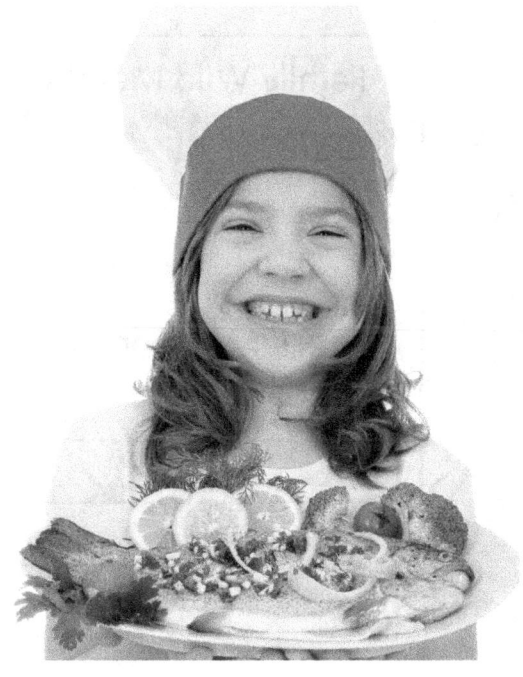

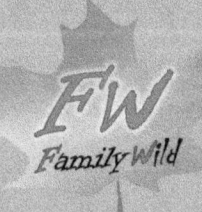
# Recipes & Food Project #1

## Family Wild Log

Member Name_____

Date_____ Time _____

Member's Age _____ Location _____

Art Project _____

Art Medium Used _____

Wildlife or Nature Included

_____

_____

_____

Family Wild Members involved (names)

_____

_____

_____

Special Memories _____

_____

_____

_____

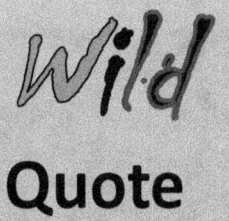
# Recipes & Food Project #2

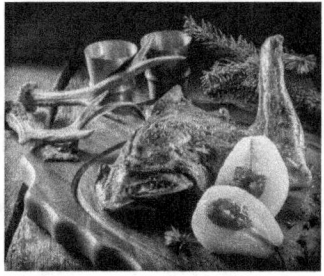

## Family Wild Log

"Food

tastes

better when

you eat it

with your

family."

Author
Unknown

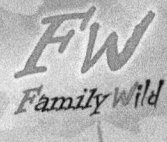

Member Name_____

Date_____ Time _____

Member's Age _____ Location _____

Art Project _____

Art Medium Used _____

Wildlife or Nature Included

_____

_____

_____

Family Wild Members involved (names)

_____

_____

_____

Special Memories _____

_____

_____

_____

_____

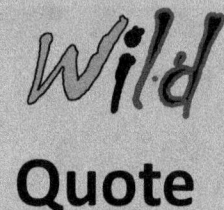
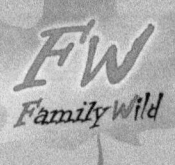
# Recipes & Food Project #3

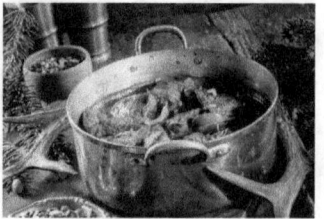

## Family Wild Log

Member Name_____

Date_____ Time _____

Member's Age _____ Location _____

Art Project _____

Art Medium Used _____

Wildlife or Nature Included

_____

_____

_____

Family Wild Members involved (names)

_____

_____

_____

Special Memories _____

_____

_____

_____

_____

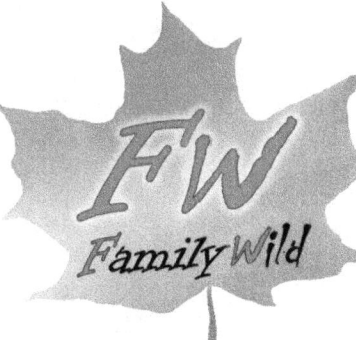

# *Family Wild*

*Herby certifies that*

_____

*Earned Family Wild's*

# Recipes & Food Slam

| | |
|---|---|
| **Date** _____ | **Project** _____ |
| **Date** _____ | **Project** _____ |
| **Date** _____ | **Project** _____ |

_____    *Michael Nunneley*

*Family Wild Local Chapter President*    *Family Wild National President*

# SLAM PICTURES

## Glue a couple pictures here

## to remember your SLAM!

You can keep the pictures in your book or put them
on the back of your certificate in a frame to
commemorate your art work!

**Below, take a few minutes to tell your story in your own words.**

Think of it as telling your grandchildren about your
art experience. It will be like sending a post card to
someone who will read it 50-100 years from now!

# My Slam Story

_____

_____

_____

_____

_____

_____

_____

# Food Plots & Gardening Slam

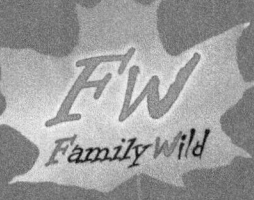

In our area, we can no longer feed deer to attract them to our box blinds due to Bovine TB. As a result, food plots and natural gardening have become critical to our deer hunting success. We've learned adding gardening for your family's consumption and enjoyment has also enriched the outdoor experience.

To qualify for this Slam, you must create at least three of the following: a wildlife food plot, clear-cut a wooded area for regeneration; plant fruit trees or berries for wildlife; create a butterfly, small game or bird habitat; or create your own garden and plant what <u>you</u> like to eat!

One thing all living things have to do is eat. You can buy feed in a bag, throw it around and wait or you can break ground, cast the seeds, fertilize and water if necessary and provide a year-round food option to your Wild animals. For those of you in northern, snowy climates, this can make the difference between your animals surviving the winter or ending up as a spring skeleton.

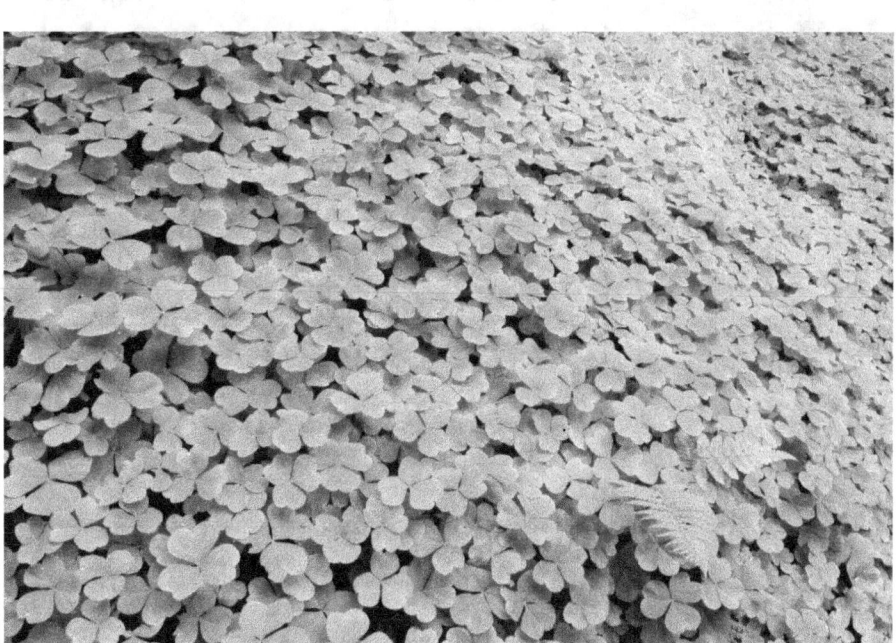

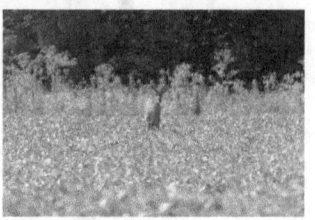

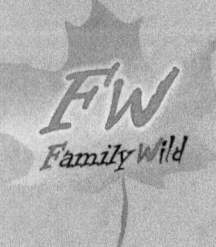

*Family Wild Log*

Member Name_____

Date_____ Time _____

Member's Age _____ Location _____

Art Project _____

Art Medium Used _____

Wildlife or Nature Included

_____

_____

_____

Family Wild Members involved (names)

_____

_____

_____

Special Memories _____

_____

_____

_____

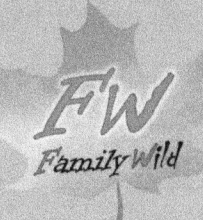
## Food Plots & Gardening #2

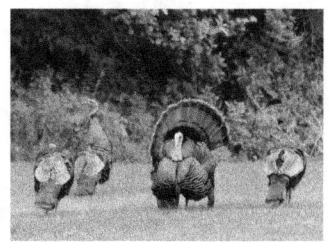

# Family Wild Log

Member Name_____

Date_____ Time _____

Member's Age _____ Location _____

Art Project _____

Art Medium Used _____

Wildlife or Nature Included

_____

_____

_____

Family Wild Members involved (names)

_____

_____

_____

Special Memories _____

_____

_____

_____

_____

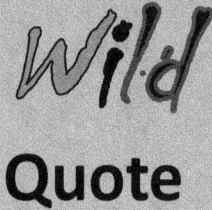

## Wild
### Quote

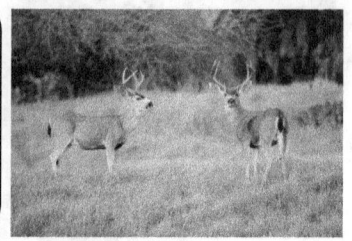

## Food Plots & Gardening #3

# Family Wild Log

Member Name _____

Date _____ Time _____

Member's Age _____ Location _____

Art Project _____

Art Medium Used _____

Wildlife or Nature Included

_____

_____

_____

_____

Family Wild Members involved (names)

_____

_____

_____

Special Memories _____

_____

_____

_____

_____

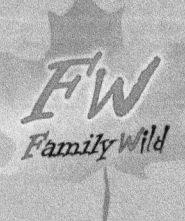

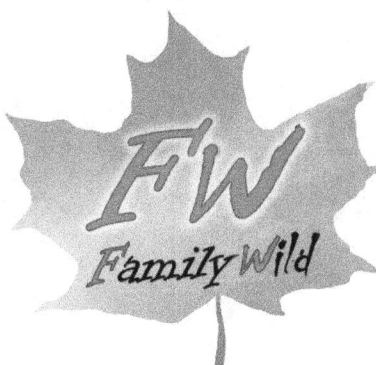

# FamilyWild

Herby certifies that

_____

## Earned FamilyWild's

# Food Plot/Gardening Slam

Date _____  Project_____

Date _____  Project_____

Date _____  Project_____

_____        *Michael Nunneley*

*FamilyWild Local Chapter President*        *FamilyWild National President*

# SLAM PICTURES

## *Glue a couple pictures here*

## *to remember your SLAM!*

You can keep the pictures in your book or put them
on the back of your certificate in a frame to
commemorate your art work!

**Below, take a few minutes to tell your story in your own words.**

Think of it as telling your grandchildren about your
art experience. It will be like sending a post card to
someone who will read it 50-100 years from now!

# My Slam Story

_____

_____

_____

_____

_____

_____

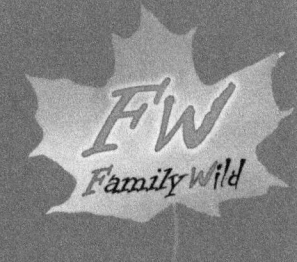

# Make Your Own Art Slam

"Be natural my children. For the writer that is natural has fulfilled all the rules of art."

**Charles Dickens** English Author

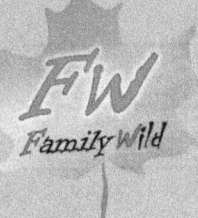

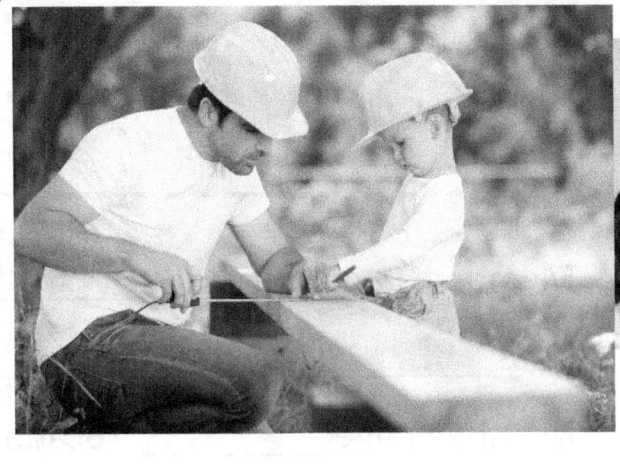

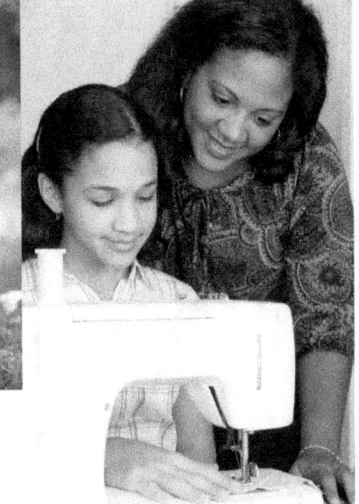

Hard as we tried, we're sure there's many more Slams to be dreamed up. So help us out! We've included this Slam for you to create. If you think it's great, send it in to us at **familywildprogram.com** and we'll take a look. We would love to add to our Slams to our second book.

The beauty of art is it's "in the eye of the beholder." If you can think of something that doesn't involve pulling a trigger or setting a hook and brings out the artist in you, then go for it and make your Slam.

Bottom line is, as with everything Family Wild, it's your club, so dream and dream *WILD!*

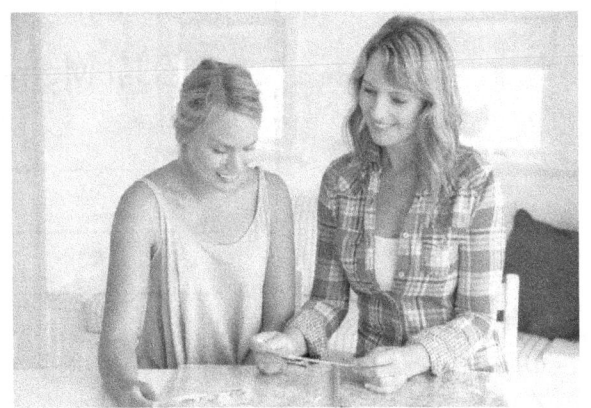

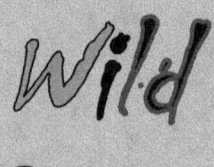

## Quote

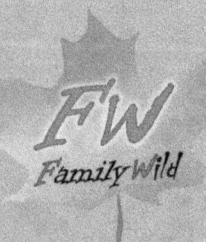

_____

# Project #1

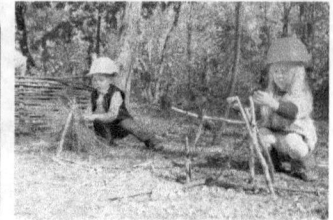

## Family Wild Log

Member Name_____

Date_____ Time _____

Member's Age _____ Location _____

Art Project _____

Art Medium Used _____

Wildlife or Nature Included

_____

_____

_____

Family Wild Members involved (names)

_____

_____

_____

Special Memories _____

_____

_____

_____

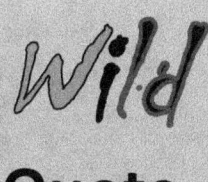

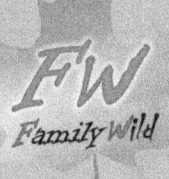
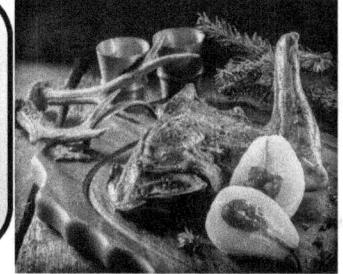

_____

# Project #2

## Family Wild Log

Member Name_____

Date_____ Time _____

Member's Age _____ Location _____

Art Project _____

Art Medium Used _____

Wildlife or Nature Included

_____

_____

_____

Family Wild Members involved (names)

_____

_____

_____

Special Memories _____

_____

_____

_____

_____

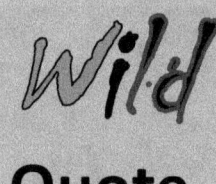
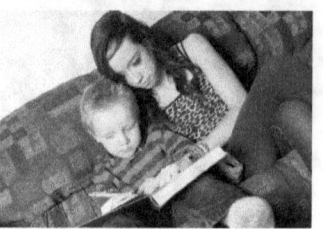

_____

# Project #3

_"Coloring outside the lines is fine art."_

## *Kim Nance*
American Actress

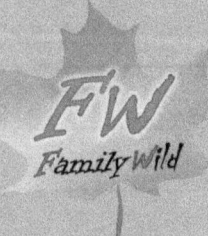

## Family Wild Log

Member Name_____

Date_____ Time _____

Member's Age _____ Location _____

Art Project _____

Art Medium Used _____

Wildlife or Nature Included

_____

_____

_____

Family Wild Members involved (names)

_____

_____

_____

Special Memories _____

_____

_____

_____

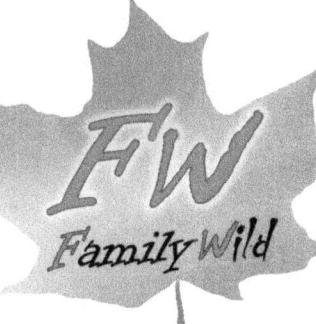

# Family Wild

*Herby certifies that*

_____

## Earned FamilyWild's

_____

**Date** _____ **Project**_____

**Date** _____ **Project** _____

**Date** _____ **Project** _____

_____                    *Michael Nunneley*

*FamilyWild Local Chapter President*          *FamilyWild National President*

# SLAM PICTURES

## Glue a couple pictures here

## to remember your SLAM!

You can keep the pictures in your book or put them
on the back of your certificate in a frame to
commemorate your art work!

**Below, take a few minutes to tell your story in your own words.**

Think of it as telling your grandchildren about your
art experience. It will be like sending a post card to
someone who will read it 50-100 years from now!

# My Slam Story

_____

_____

_____

_____

_____

_____

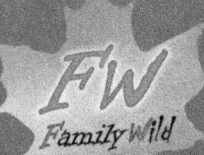
# Family Wild

## Chapter
## 7
## Family Wild
## Lifetime Slams

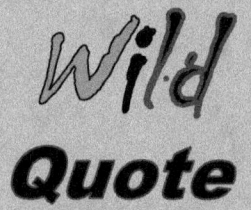

## Wild Quote

# Lifetime Slams

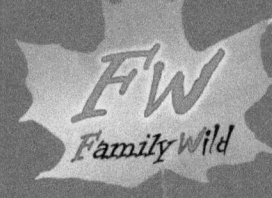

*"Unless (artists) can remember what it was like to be a little boy, they are only half complete as artist and man."*

**James Thurber** American Cartoonist

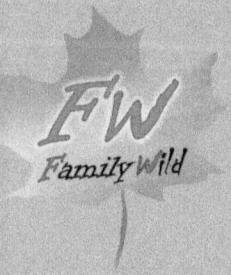

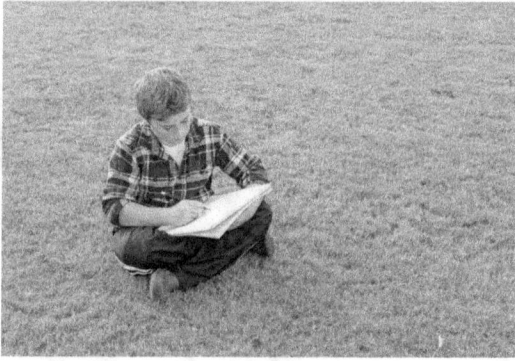

As Luke Bryan says "Hunting, Fishing, Loving Every Day..." Family Wild offers our Slams for hunting, fishing and nature-art activities involving our North American outdoors. With a lifetime of outdoor activities to choose, you and your young members can strive to earn our Lifetime Slams.

We have three Lifetime Slams that require you to earn four, eight, and twelve individual Slams to achieve the Grand, Super and ULTIMATE Activity Slams.

If you happen to love hunting or fishing, check out our other Family Wild Hunting & Fishing Handbooks. You can earn Hunting and Fishing Slams similar to the nature art Slams in this book. Again, earn four, eight, or twelve individual Hunting or Fishing Slams and you've earned our Hunting or Fishing Lifetime Slams!

Finally, for the complete outdoor fanatic, if you live for Hunting, Fishing and Loving Everyday, chase the WILD LIFETIME SLAMS! You have to earn <u>eight</u> slams in at least two different categories of Hunting, Fishing and Nature Art to achieve the WILD GRAND SLAM. You can then work toward <u>sixteen</u> hunting, fishing or activity slams to capture the WILD SUPER SLAM.

Don't stop now! You've nearly achieved the WILD ULTIMATE SLAM!!! Earn the pinnacle of the Family Wild SLAMS when you earn a total of <u>twenty-four</u> art, hunting and fishing activity slams. Now you understand why we said these were *Family Wild* Lifetime Achievements!

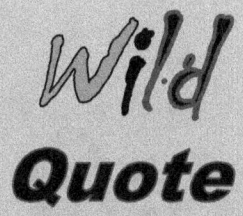

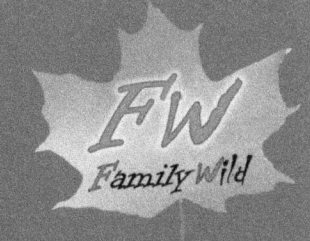
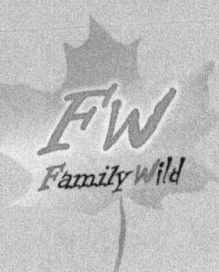
## Family Wild

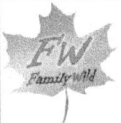 **Art Grand Slam**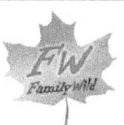

This Slam requires you to earn at least **Four Art** slams!

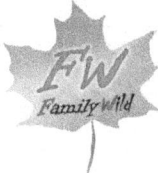 **Art**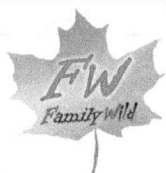

**Super Slam**

This Slam requires you to earn at least **Eight Art** slams!

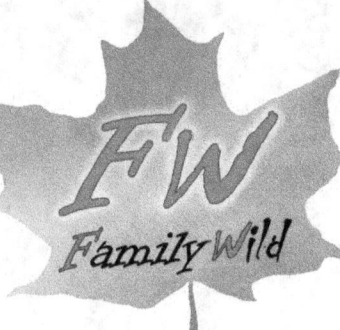

# Family Wild

*Herby certifies that*

_____

*Earned Family Wild's*

# ART

# GRAND SLAM

## Art Slams Achieved

Date _____  Slam _____

Date _____  Slam _____

Date _____  Slam _____

Date _____  Slam _____

_____  *Michael Nunneley*

*Family Wild Local Chapter President*  *Family Wild National President*

# SLAM PICTURES

## Glue a couple pictures here

## to remember your SLAM!

You can keep the pictures in your book or put them
on the back of your certificate in a frame to
commemorate your art work!

**Below, take a few minutes to tell your story in your own words.**

Think of it as telling your grandchildren about your
art experience. It will be like sending a post card to
someone who will read it 50-100 years from now!

# My Slam Story

_____

_____

_____

_____

_____

_____

_____

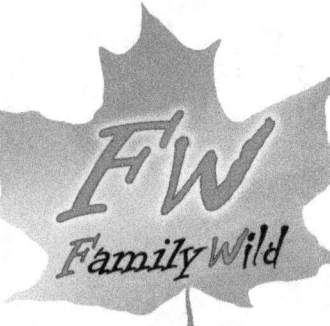

# Family Wild

*Herby certifies that*

_____

*Earned Family Wild's*

# ART
# SUPER SLAM

## Art Slams Achieved

Date _____ Slam _____     Date _____ Slam _____

Date _____ Slam _____     Date _____ Slam _____

Date _____ Slam _____     Date _____ Slam _____

Date _____ Slam _____     Date _____ Slam _____

*Michael Nunneley*

_____

*FamilyWild Local Chapter President*     *FamilyWild National President*

## SLAM PICTURES

### Glue a couple pictures here
### to remember your SLAM!

You can keep the pictures in your book or put them
on the back of your certificate in a frame to
commemorate your art work!

**Below, take a few minutes to tell your story in your own words.**

Think of it as telling your grandchildren about your
art experience. It will be like sending a post card to
someone who will read it 50-100 years from now!

## My Slam Story

_____

_____

_____

_____

_____

_____

_____

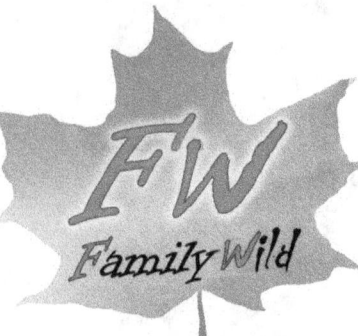

# Family Wild

### Herby certifies that

---

## Earned Family Wild's

# ART
# ULTIMATE SLAM

### Art Slams Achieved

Date _____ Slam _____          Date _____ Slam _____

Date _____ Slam _____          Date _____ Slam _____

Date _____ Slam _____          Date _____ Slam _____

Date _____ Slam _____          Date _____ Slam _____

Date _____ Slam _____          Date _____ Slam _____

Date _____ Slam _____          Date _____ Slam _____

Date _____ Slam _____          Date _____ Slam _____

Date _____ Slam _____          Date _____ Slam _____

*Michael Nunneley*

_____

Family Wild Local Chapter President          Family Wild National President

# SLAM PICTURES

## *Glue a couple pictures here*
## *to remember your SLAM!*

You can keep the pictures in your book or put them
on the back of your certificate in a frame to
commemorate your art work!

**Below, take a few minutes to tell your story in your own words.**

Think of it as telling your grandchildren about your
art experience. It will be like sending a post card to
someone who will read it 50-100 years from now!

## My Slam Story

_____

_____

_____

_____

_____

_____

_____

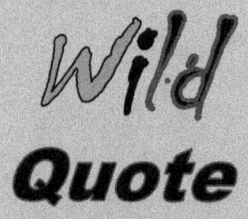

# Wild Quote

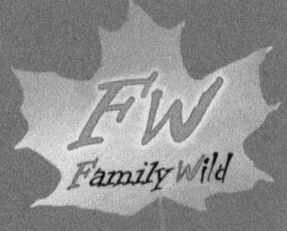

"Anybody who keeps the ability to see beauty never grows old."

**Franki Kafka** German Novelist

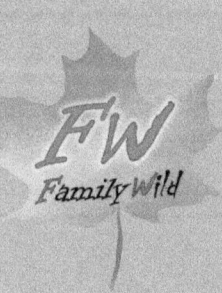

## Family Wild

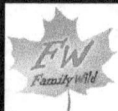

## The WILD Grand Slam

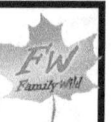

This Slam requires you to earn at least **Eight** Art, Fishing or Hunting Slams!

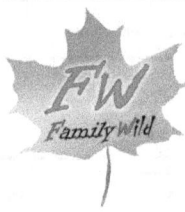

## The WILD Super Slam

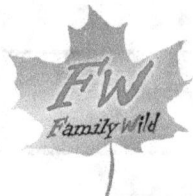

This Slam requires you to earn at least **Sixteen** Art, Fishing or Hunting Slams!

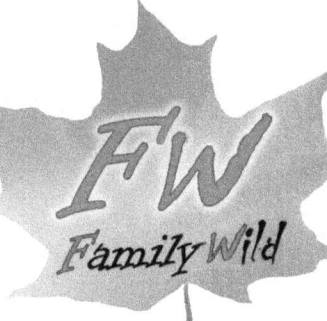

# *Family Wild*

*Herby certifies that*

_____

## *Earned Family Wild's*

# WILD
# GRAND SLAM

### Slams Achieved

| | |
|---|---|
| *Date* _____ | *Slam* _____ |
| *Date* _____ | *Slam* _____ |
| *Date* _____ | *Slam* _____ |
| *Date* _____ | *Slam* _____ |
| *Date* _____ | *Slam* _____ |
| *Date* _____ | *Slam* _____ |
| *Date* _____ | *Slam* _____ |
| *Date* _____ | *Slam* _____ |

*Michael Nunneley*

_____

*Family Wild Local Chapter President*      *Family Wild National President*

# SLAM PICTURES

## Glue a couple pictures here

## to remember your SLAM!

You can keep the pictures in your book or put them
on the back of your certificate in a frame to
commemorate your art work!

**Below, take a few minutes to tell your story in your own words.**

Think of it as telling your grandchildren about your
art experience. It will be like sending a post card to
someone who will read it 50-100 years from now!

## My Slam Story

_____

_____

_____

_____

_____

_____

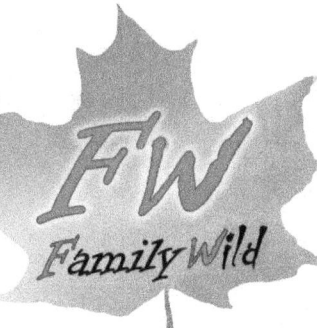

# Family Wild

*Herby certifies that*

_____

*Earned Family Wild's*

# WILD
# SUPER SLAM

## Combined Family Wild Slams

Date _____ Slam _____     Date _____ Slam _____
Date _____ Slam _____     Date _____ Slam _____
Date _____ Slam _____     Date _____ Slam _____
Date _____ Slam _____     Date _____ Slam _____
Date _____ Slam _____     Date _____ Slam _____
Date _____ Slam _____     Date _____ Slam _____
Date _____ Slam _____     Date _____ Slam _____
Date _____ Slam _____     Date _____ Slam _____

*Michael Nunneley*

_____
*Family Wild Local Chapter President*     *Family Wild National President*

# SLAM PICTURES

## Glue a couple pictures here

## to remember your SLAM!

You can keep the pictures in your book or put them
on the back of your certificate in a frame to
commemorate your art work!

**Below, take a few minutes to tell your story in your own words.**

Think of it as telling your grandchildren about your
art experience. It will be like sending a post card to
someone who will read it 50-100 years from now!

## My Slam Story

_____

_____

_____

_____

_____

_____

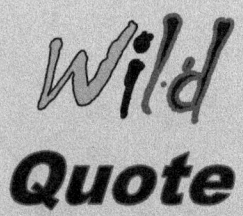

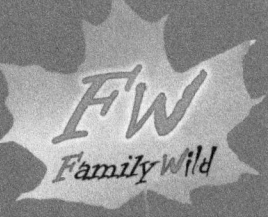

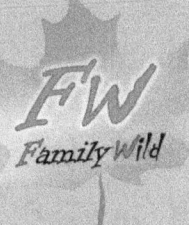

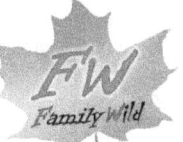 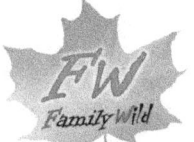 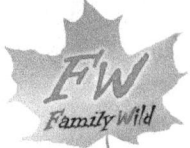

# *Family Wild*

# ULTIMATE

# Slam

This Slam requires you

to earn at least

## Twenty-four

*Family Wild* Slams

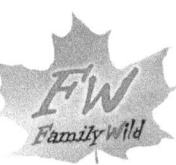 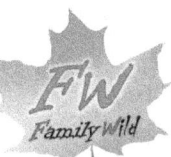 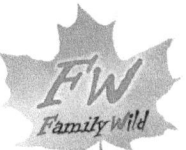

# Family Wild

## Herby certifies that

_____

## Earned Family Wild's

# WILD
# ULTIMATE SLAM

### Slams Achieved

| Date _____ Slam _____ | Date _____ Slam _____ |
|---|---|
| Date _____ Slam _____ | Date _____ Slam _____ |
| Date _____ Slam _____ | Date _____ Slam _____ |
| Date _____ Slam _____ | Date _____ Slam _____ |
| Date _____ Slam _____ | Date _____ Slam _____ |
| Date _____ Slam _____ | Date _____ Slam _____ |
| Date _____ Slam _____ | Date _____ Slam _____ |
| Date _____ Slam _____ | Date _____ Slam _____ |
| Date _____ Slam _____ | Date _____ Slam _____ |
| Date _____ Slam _____ | Date _____ Slam _____ |
| Date _____ Slam _____ | Date _____ Slam _____ |

_Michael Nunneley_

_____

Family Wild Local Chapter President

Family Wild National President

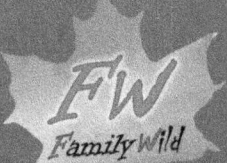
# Family Wild

# Chapter
# 8
# Family Wild's
# Highest Honor

# Wild
## Quote

# Teddy Roosevelt
## "Walk Softly"
### Circle of Honor

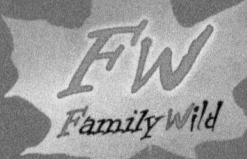

"I recognize the right and duty of this generation to develop and use the natural resources of our land; but I do not recognize the right to waste them, or to rob, by wasteful use, the generations that come after us. "

**Theodore "Teddy" Roosevelt**
*26th President*

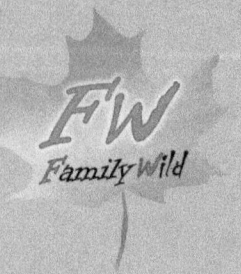

## Family Wild's
# Highest Honor

According to the US National Park Service Webpage

https://www.nps.gov/thro/learn/historyculture/theodore-roosevelt-and-conservation.htm

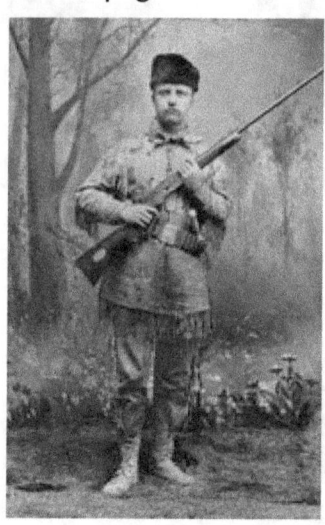

*Theodore Roosevelt is often considered the "conservationist president." In the North Dakota Badlands, where many of his personal concerns first gave rise to his later environmental efforts, Roosevelt is remembered with a national park that bears his name and honors the memory of this great conservationist.*

**"We have fallen heirs to the most glorious heritage a people ever received, and each one must do his part if we wish to show that the nation is worthy of its good fortune."**

**Theodore "Teddy" Roosevelt**
*26th President of the United States*

President Roosevelt challenged Americans to maintain the great natural resources of our land. As a result, *Family Wild* honors President Roosevelt's hunting and conservation legacy with our HIGHEST HONOR.

To earn membership into the **Teddy Roosevelt "Walk Softly" Conservation Circle of Honor** your *Family Wild Club* must do your part to improve our North American lands. Although we all can't be President of the United States or the Canadian Prime Minister, everyone of us can make our environment better than we found it.

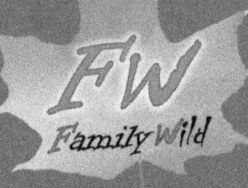
"Of all the questions which can come before this nation, short of the actual preservation of its existence in a great war, there is none which compares in importance with the great central task of leaving this land even a better land for our descendants than it is for us."

**Theodore "Teddy" Roosevelt**
*26th President*

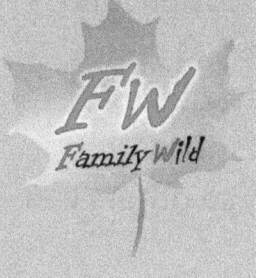

## Family Wild's
# Highest Honor

The National Park Service Website continues-

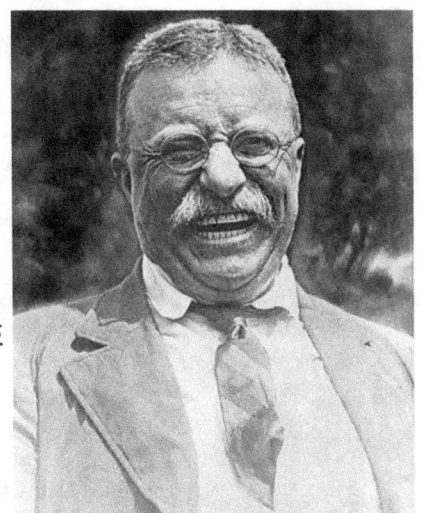

*The decimation of bison, and the eradication of elk, bighorn sheep, deer and other game species was a loss which Roosevelt felt indicative of society's perception of our natural resources. He saw the effects of overgrazing, and suffered the <u>loss of his ranches</u> because of it. While many still considered natural resources inexhaustible, Roosevelt would write:*

**"We have become great because of the lavish use of our resources. But the time has come to inquire seriously what will happen when our forests are gone, when the coal, the iron, the oil, and the gas are exhausted, when the soils have still further impoverished and washed into the streams, polluting the rivers, denuding the fields and obstructing navigation."**

**Theodore "Teddy" Roosevelt**
*26th President of the United States*

*Conservation increasingly became one of Roosevelt's main concerns. After becoming president in 1901, Roosevelt used his authority to protect wildlife and public lands by creating the United States Forest Service (USFS) and establishing 150 national forests, 51 federal bird reserves, 4 national game preserves, 5 national parks, and 18 national monuments by enabling the <u>1906 American Antiquities Act</u>. During his presidency, Republican Theodore Roosevelt protected approximately 230 million acres of public land.*

## Wild Quote

# Teddy Roosevelt "Walk Softly"
### Circle of Honor continued

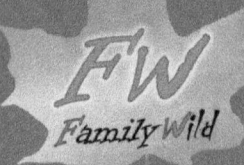

"There are no words that can tell the hidden spirit of the wilderness, that can reveal its mystery, its melancholy and its charm."

**Theodore "Teddy" Roosevelt**
*26th President*

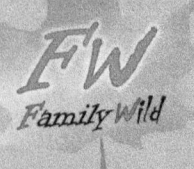

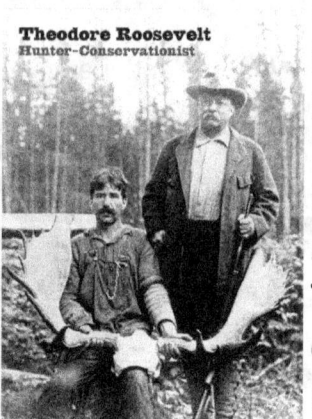

Please understand, we expect all *Family Wild* clubs and members to leave our environment better than you found it. If you find garbage in the woods, pick it up and dispose of it properly. If you find trash floating in a lake, river or stream grab it and throw it out.

However, to enter the exclusive *Family Wild's* Highest Honor-the **Teddy Roosevelt "Walk Softly" Circle of Honor**-your club must complete a project that improves the environment in a substantial way.

You will need to capture "before" pictures/video of your project area, showing us the condition of the environment you want to improve. You need to document your project through photos and videos illustrating the efforts of your members to pursue your groups environmental improvements.

You will need to keep a record of a minimum of 80 club hours on your project. This needs to reflect each members verified contribution to your team's efforts.

You will need to write down the daily progress of your project -indicating the "high" and the "lows" as you move along. Keep in mind, you're setting the stage for others to replicate your project. As a result, make sure you indicate what worked and what didn't, so others can benefit from your experience.

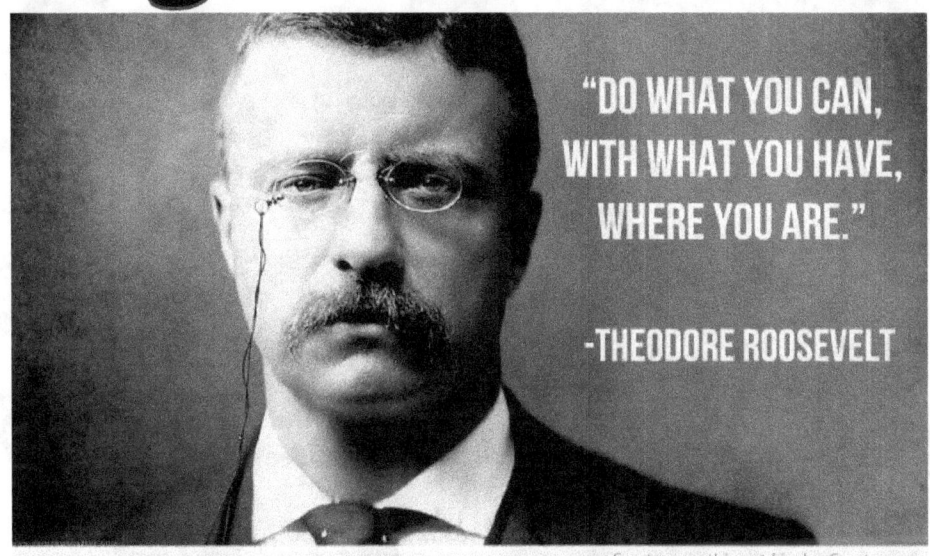
**"The farther one gets into the wilderness, the greater is the attraction of its lonely freedom."**

**Theodore "Teddy" Roosevelt**
*26th President*

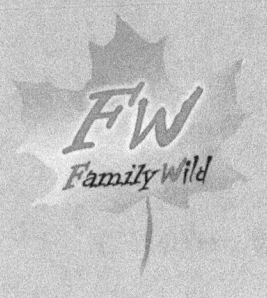

# Family Wild's
# Highest Honor

"DO WHAT YOU CAN, WITH WHAT YOU HAVE, WHERE YOU ARE."

-THEODORE ROOSEVELT

Create something at LiveLuvCreate.com

Teddy Roosevelt made famous the term "Bully Pulpit." For Teddy, the word bully, meant "superb" or "wonderful," and the White House afforded him the platform to announce to the world his thoughts and visions.

As a result, in the memory of President Roosevelt, you need to let the world know your accomplishments. You'll need to document your press releases, press conference and submit to us any publications and report/describe radio and television news broadcasts that featured your story. Don't be shy - someone in your club can answer questions from the media to celebrate your family's accomplishment.

We understand that many folks don't like to toot their own horn. However, by publicly announcing your efforts you set the example for others to follow with projects of their own.

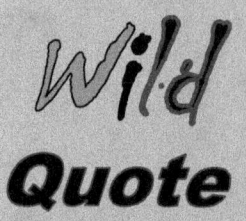

# Teddy Roosevelt
# "Walk Softly"
## Circle of Honor continued

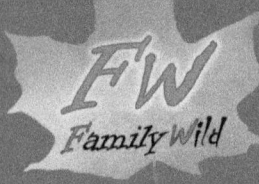

## Wild Quote

"Each time we face our fear, we gain strength, courage, and confidence in the doing."

**Theodore "Teddy" Roosevelt**
*26th President*

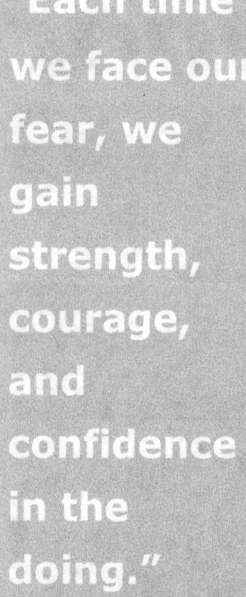

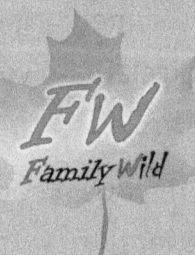

# Family Wild's
# Highest Honor

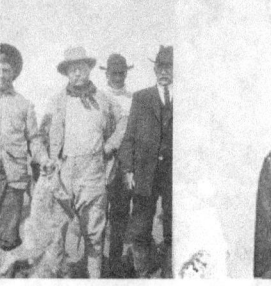
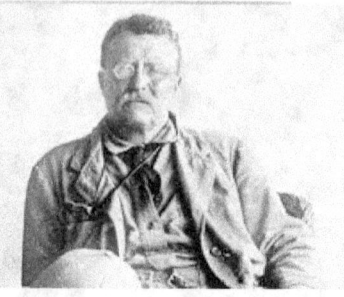
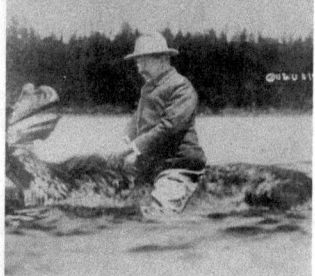

We ask that you work with your children to submit a 1000-2000 word essay about your project. We want you to document the following themes:

**Where did your idea originate?**

What materials did you use?

**Who helped and what was their relationship to the family. How old were the participants?**

How long did your project take?

**Describe the "highlight moment" of your project.**

What would you do differently?

**Who will your project benefit? Explain.**

Did you partner with others? Did others donate time, materials? If so, who and what?

**What future efforts are required to maintain your project?**

What did you do to promote your project's results?

**How were the results and what would you do differently?**

## Teddy Roosevelt
# "Walk Softly"
### Circle of Honor continued

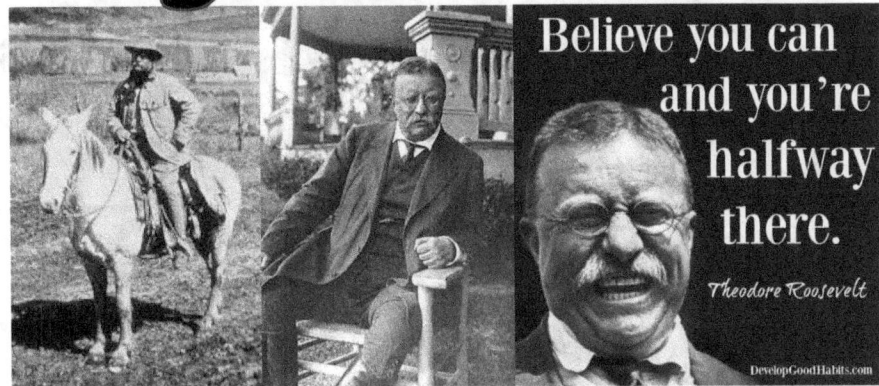

# Family Wild's Highest Honor

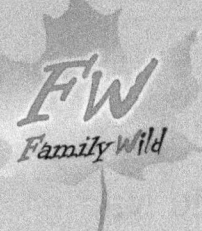

We also ask that you work with your children to submit a 500 word essay about President Teddy Roosevelt. For your topic, pick a Roosevelt quote or historical fact you found interesting.

Please convey the quote or fact, when it occurred, and where it occurred. Describe why your group chose that quote or fact and what it meant to you in relation to your project.

Explain the impact President Roosevelt had on the sports of hunting, conservation, and/or the National Park System.

So often we don't take time to remember our history and those who saved and respected the natural resources we enjoy today. The original premise of *Family Wild* was to bring children, parents, and grandparents together to make time to pass on life experiences from one generation to the next.

Enjoy learning about one of America's most intriguing Presidents and the Father of American Conservation - Teddy Roosevelt.

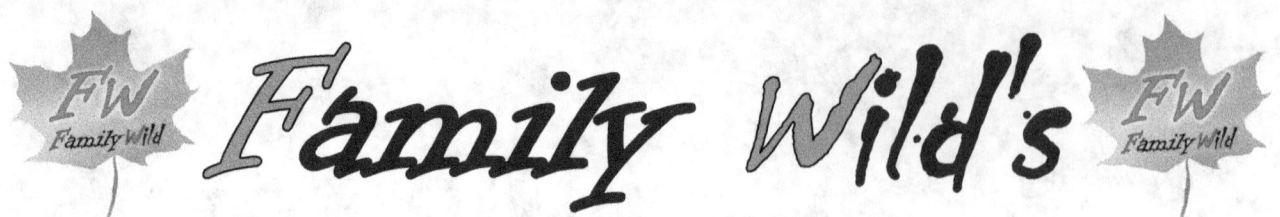

# Teddy Roosevelt
# "Walk Softly"
## Circle of Honor
## Application

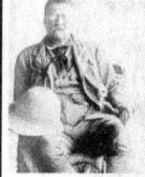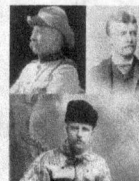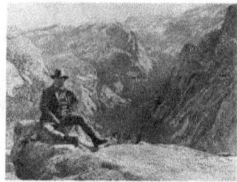

Application Date _____

Family Wild Group Name _____

Group Contact Person _____

Address _____ _____ _____
       Street Address          State    Zip Code

Contact Phone Number _____

Contact E-Mail _____

## Items Needed for Application:

**Before Pictures** _____          **During Pictures** _____

**After Pictures** _____          **Press Documents** _____

**Volunteer Hours Report** _____          **Roosevelt Essay** _____

**Project Essay** _____

_____          _____

Contact Signature          Contact Printed Name

# *Walk Softly PICTURES*

## *Glue a couple pictures here*

## *to remember your Walk Softly Project.*

You can keep the pictures in your book or put them
on the back of your certificate in a frame to
commemorate your project years from now!

**Below, take a few minutes to tell your story in your own words.**

Think of it as telling your grandchildren about your
project experience. It will be like a sending a post card
Someone will read 50-100 years from now!

# Our Walk Softly Story

_____

_____

_____

_____

_____

_____

## *Walk Softly PICTURES*

### *Glue a couple pictures here*

### *to remember your Walk Softly Project.*

You can keep the pictures in your book or put them
on the back of your certificate in a frame to
commemorate your project years from now!

**Below, take a few minutes to tell your story in your own words.**

Think of it as telling your grandchildren about your
project experience. It will be like a sending a post card
Someone will read 50-100 years from now!

# Our Walk Softly Story

_____

_____

_____

_____

_____

_____

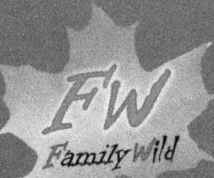
# *Family Wild*

# Appendix

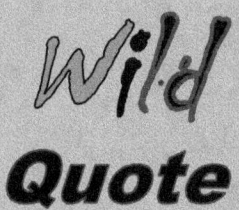

# Appendix

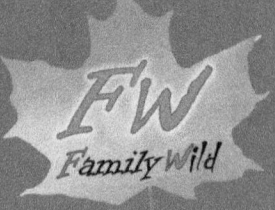

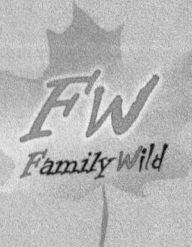
## Family Wild

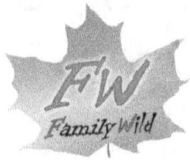 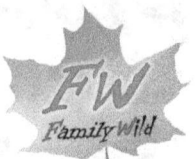 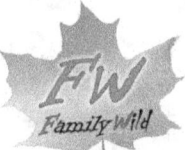

## More Cool Stuff

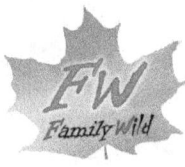 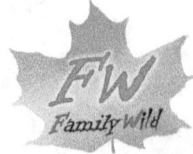 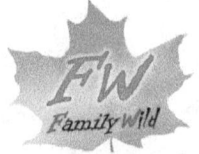

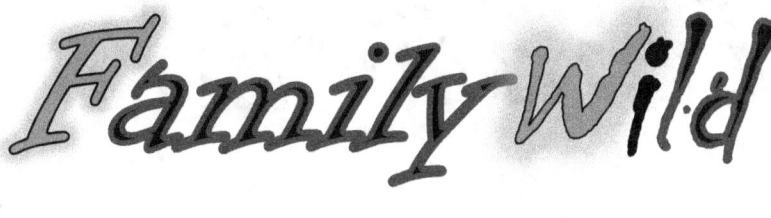

# First Annual Art Show!

## Date: _____

## Time: _____

## Location:_____

Congratulations! We have selected you and your family to participate in our First Annual Family Wild Art Show. Prepare yourself for a day of food, fun and memories! Bring your entire family and a dish to pass for everyone's enjoyment.

We'll have certificates (or trophies) for our various Art Show Winners. Plus we'll have some art supply awards! At the end of the Show we'll have an Awards Ceremony and then dinner!!! One rule for all-Come and Have Fun!!!


Sincerely,


**Family Wild President**

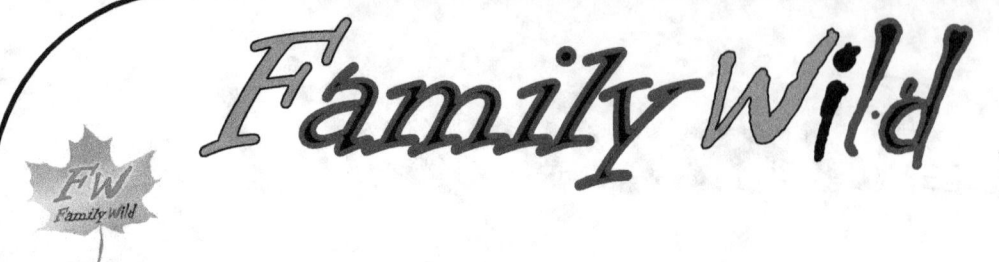

# First Annual Art Show

| Name | Address | Phone | Email |
|------|---------|-------|-------|
|      |         |       |       |
|      |         |       |       |
|      |         |       |       |
|      |         |       |       |
|      |         |       |       |
|      |         |       |       |
|      |         |       |       |
|      |         |       |       |
|      |         |       |       |
|      |         |       |       |
|      |         |       |       |
|      |         |       |       |
|      |         |       |       |
|      |         |       |       |
|      |         |       |       |

# Sign in Sheet

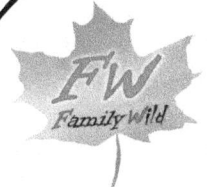 *Family Wild*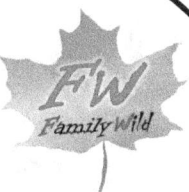

# First Annual
# Art Show!

## Saturday

## August 15, 2016

## 9:00 A.M.-3:00 P.M.

*Registration  8 A.M. - 10 P.M*

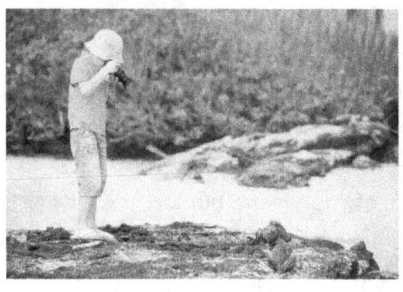

*Awards
at
4:00 P.M.*

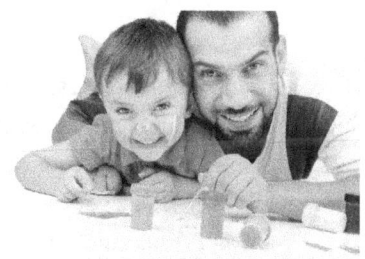

**Registration, Check in & Awards at the Pavilion**

**1111 S. State St. Alpena, MI  49707**

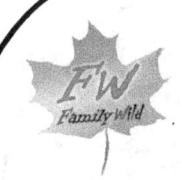
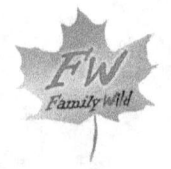

# Family Wild

# Art Show Press Release

**To:** (All area Newspapers, Radio Stations, TV Stations, Free Weekly Advertiser Paper, other Hunting, Fishing & Art Groups - **contact them all and save the emails or faxes. Also, look on their websites for direct contact drop downs and then save for future use**)

**From:** Alpena Chapter of Family Wild

**Re:** First annual Family Art Show Results

The **Family Wild** Chapter of Alpena recently concluded their First Annual **Family Wild** Art Show in the Alpena area with 42 artists participating. Young John Brown took First Place in the Children Photography division. Sally Black earned First in the Adult Division and George Jones captured the Grandparents division.

Courtney White won the Children's Painting division and Jack Jones the Adult Division. The videography division winners whereas Ian Hope and Robbie Martin. The winner of the Drawing Division was Rick Donald. The Sculpture winner was Graham Mark.

Family Wild would like to thank sponsors MC Sports, Dunham's, Wal-Mart, Clem's Bait & Tackle, Bucks Bait and Meijer's for their generous support of our **Family Wild** Annual Art Show. Visit the **Family Wild** Alpena Chapter Website for additional club information and details about next years event at www.familywildalpenachapter.com.

Feel free to change any of the wording of this Sample Results Press Release to fit your event. **AGAIN!!!** Most important, make sure you get the word out. Make this a big deal, even if you're just starting your event. Make sure to get as many people recognized as possible. Make sure you get the results out as soon as possible. The longer you wait, the less likely you'll get covered. We know you'll feel tired at the end of your event, but try and get results out the same day. People of all ages love to have their names and/or pictures in the paper or on the news. Make it sound big and fun and you'll get coverage. Go For It! Also, include pictures (make sure you have singed Photo Releases – we have included the blank forms) so you can use them on your Facebook page, website or blog and to help promote next year's event.

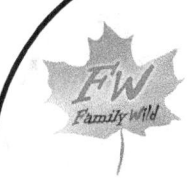
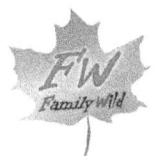

# Family Wild

# Adult Photo Release

I hereby authorize **Family Wild** Alpena Chapter hereafter referred to as the "Company" to publish photographs taken of me on August 15 2016 and my name and likeness, for use in the **Family Wild** Alpena Chapters print, online and video-based marketing materials, press releases, as well as any other Company publications.

I hereby release and hold harmless **Family Wild** Alpena Chapter from any reasonable expectation of privacy or confidentiality associated with the images specified above.

I further acknowledge that my voluntary participation and that I will not receive financial compensation of any type associated with the taking or publications of these photographs or participation in company marketing materials or other Company publications. I acknowledge and agree that publications of said photos confers no rights of ownership or royalties whatsoever.

I hereby release **Family Wild** Alpena Chapter, its contractors, its employees and any third parties involved in the creation or publication of marketing materials, from liability for any claims by me or any third party in connection with my participation.

Authorization:    Printed Name _____

Signature _____

Address_____

Feel free to use this sample Photo Release form or check with your own attorney for their recommendations. We live in a sue-happy society. DON'T take for granted that everyone wants their picture published. Cover all your bases and your backside and have everyone fill out this form as part of REGISTRATION. That way, you'll know **before** you take pictures/video and publicize them who wants DOESN'T want to see themselves in the paper, on the news or on your website. As a former professional photographer, I know you want this form as part of your registration packet! **BETTER SAFE THAN SORRY!**

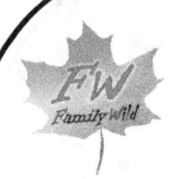 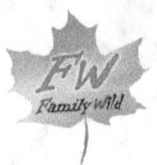

# *Family Wild*

# Adult/Minor Child Photo Release

I hereby authorize Family Wild Alpena Chapter hereafter referred to as the "Company" to publish photographs taken of me on October August and likenesses, for use in the Family Wild Alpena Chapters print, online and video-based marketing materials, press releases, as well as any other Company publications.

I hereby release and hold harmless Family Wild Alpena Chapter from any reasonable expectation of privacy or confidentiality of myself and my minor children associated with the images specified above. Further, I attest that I am the parent or legal guardian of the child or children listed below and that I have full authority to consent and authorize Family Wild Alpena Chapter to use their likeness and names.

I further acknowledge that my voluntary participation and that I, the minor child or children, will not receive financial compensation of any type associated with the taking or publications of these photographs or participation in company marketing materials or other Company publications. I acknowledge and agree that publications of said photos confers no rights of ownership or royalties whatsoever.

I hereby release Family Wild Alpena Chapter, its contractors, its employees and any third parties involved in the creation or publication of marketing materials, from liability for any claims by me or any third party in connection with my participation or the minor children listed below.

Authorization:     Printed Name _____

                    Signature _____

                    Address_____

Names and Ages of Minor Children

                    Name_____ Age _____

                    Name_____ Age _____

Feel free to use this sample Minor Child Photo Release form or check with your own attorney for their recommendations. Have every parent/guardian fill this out at registration. **AGAIN-BETTER SAFE THAN SORRY!**

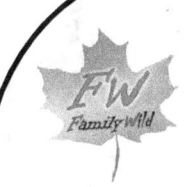 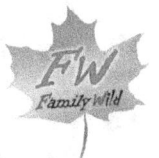

# *Family Wild*

# Intellectual Property Release Form

INTELLECTUAL PROPERTY RELEASE FORM-I authorize **Family Wild, LLC** to use copyright materials, images, recordings, names or personal information of the following:

_____ the undersigned, understand that I own the copyright on any materials I've provided to **Family Wild, LLC,** and I can, if I so wish, grant permission to others the right to publish materials I produce. I, therefore, do hereby grant to: **Family Wild, LLC,** its successors, and assigns, the absolute unlimited right to use and/or publish photographs, video, print, electronic or any other media, or intellectual property, the following materials as originally produced unless a written agreement detailing any changes to the materials is obtained between me and **Family Wild, LLC** to which I am providing consent.

Attached to this consent form are the original materials to which I am providing consent to use and any written agreement regarding changes to the original materials. **(Description of materials attached to this form)** I hereby warrant I am the author/ owner/publisher of the materials I am providing and/or that I have obtained all necessary legal rights and permissions to use the materials and/or convey their use to others. The permission I have obtained and assigned to above-named organization is limited to using the materials as originally produced unless a written agreement is obtained between me and the above-named organization to alter the materials and in which all changes to the original materials will be noted.

I hereby warrant that I am of full legal age and have the right to contract in my own name. I have read the above authorization, release and agreement prior to its execution, am fully familiar with and understand the contents thereof, and agree to its terms knowingly and voluntarily. This consent and release shall be binding upon me and my heirs, legal representatives, and assigns.

_____          _____

          (Print Name)                            Signature

Date _____

# Family Wild

FW Family Wild

FW Family Wild

Herby certifies that

_____

Earned 1st Place in

# Photography

Date _____

_Michael Nunneley_
Family Wild National President

_____
Family Wild Local Chapter President

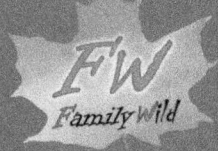 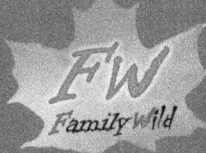

**BYLAWS OF FAMILY WILD-** _____ **Chapter**

## ARTICLE I - NAME AND PURPOSE

**Section 1 - Name:** The name of the organization shall be **Family Wild -** _____ **Chapter.** It shall be a nonprofit organization organized under the laws of the State of _____.

**Section 2 - Purpose:** Family Wild – _____ **Chapter** organized exclusively for charitable, scientific and education purposes. The purpose of this organization shall support and conduct research, education, and informational activities to encourage family activities, bonding and memories while experiencing, managing and improving outdoor resources through hunting, fishing activities, habitat management and the arts.

## ARTICLE II - MEMBERSHIP

**Section 1 -** Eligibility for membership: Application for voting membership shall be open to any current member or friend of the _____ family that supports the purpose statement in Article I, Section 2. Membership occurs after completion and receipt of a membership application. All memberships shall occur upon a majority vote of the board.

**Section 2 - Annual dues**: The amount required for annual dues shall be $_____ each year, unless changed by a majority vote of the members at an annual meeting of the full membership. Membership continues upon submitting up-to-date on membership dues.

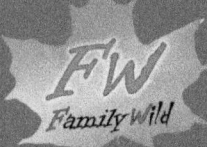 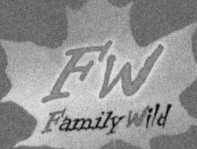

# By-Laws

**BYLAWS OF FAMILY WILD-** _____ **Chapter**

**Section 3 - Rights of members:**  Each member in good standing, regardless of age, shall be eligible to vote. Membership in *Family Wild* - Chapter _____ comes with lifelong rights, privileges and responsibilities as outlined within these by-laws.

## ARTICLE III - MEETINGS OF MEMBERS

**Section 1 - Regular meetings**:  Regular meetings of the members shall be held weekly, monthly or quarterly, at a time and place designated by the chair.

**Section 2 - Annual meetings:**  An annual meeting of the members shall take place in the month of October, the specific date, time and location of which will be designated by the chair. At the annual meeting, the members shall elect directors and officers, receive reports on the activities of the club, and determine the direction of the club for the coming year.

**Section 3 - Special meetings**:  Special meetings may be called by the chair, the Executive Committee, or any member of the board of directors.

**Section 4 - Notice of meetings:**  Shall be conveyed at the Dinner Table, by phone, text or email to all members as to allow enough time for attendance.

**Section 5 - Quorum:**  The members present at any properly announced meeting shall constitute a quorum.

**Section 6 - Voting:**  All issues to be voted on shall be decided by a simple majority of those present at the meeting in which the vote takes place.

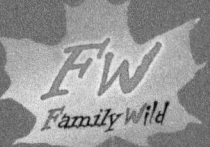

**BYLAWS OF FAMILY WILD-** _____**Chapter**

## ARTICLE IV - BOARD OF DIRECTORS

**Section 1 - Board role, size, and compensation**: Responsible for overall policy and direction of the club, the Board delegates responsibility of day-to-day operations to the members and committees. The board shall have up to 7, but not fewer than 3 members. The board receives no compensation other than respect and admiration and the occasional thank you from the membership.

**Section 2 - Terms:** All board members shall serve a two-year term, but remain eligible for re-election for up to five consecutive terms.

**Section 3 - Meetings and notice:** The board shall meet at least quarterly, at an agreed upon time and place. An official board meeting requires that each board member have written/emailed/texted notice at least two days in advance.

**Section 4 - Board elections**: New directors and current directors shall be elected or re-elected by the voting representatives of members at the annual meeting. Directors will be elected by a simple majority of members present at the annual meeting.

**Section 5 - Election procedures:** Any member can nominate a candidate or offer themselves as a candidate to the slate of nominees.

**Section 6 - Quorum:** A quorum must be attended by at least fifty percent of membership for business transactions to take place and motions to pass. A non-profit with voting members should hold at least one meeting of its members per year. Unless otherwise specified by the articles or bylaws, ten percent of the members entitled to vote at the meeting results in a quorum or attendance requirements in accordance to *(your State)* law.

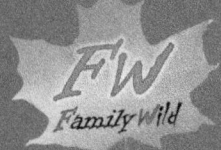

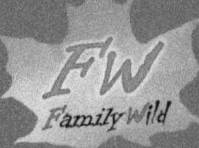

**BYLAWS OF FAMILY WILD-** _____Chapter

**Section 7 - Officers and Duties:** There shall be six officers of the board, consisting of a President, Vice-President, Secretary, Treasurer, Historian and PR Director. Their duties follow:

**The President** shall convene regularly scheduled board meetings, shall preside or arrange for other members of the Executive Committee to preside at each meeting in the following order: Vice-President, Secretary, Treasurer, Historian and PR Director.

**The Vice-President** shall chair committees on special subjects as designated by the board. Further, the Vice-President shall preside in the absence of the President.

**The Secretary** shall be responsible for keeping records of board actions, including overseeing the taking of minutes at all board meetings, sending out member communications, and assuring maintenance of corporate records.

**The Treasurer** shall make a report at each board meeting. The Treasurer shall chair the finance committee, assist in the preparation of the budget, help develop fundraising plans, and make financial information available to board members and the public.

**The Historian** shall create, maintain and preserve documentation, photos and videos of all activities of the **_Family Wild_** – Chapter _____ for the enjoyment of generations for years to come.

**The PR Director** shall create a social media space (webpage, Facebook account) as well as publicize events in any way seen fit by the board to further document and publicize upcoming and recent events of the club. We recommend a young, tech savvy member of the club familiar with social media, text, Facebook, Twitter, and overall computer and smart phone technologies (in other words you probably won't select Grandpa or Grandma for this position – but you might!)

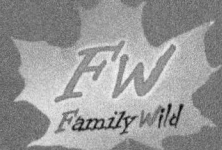 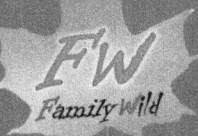

**BYLAWS OF FAMILY WILD-** _____**Chapter**

**Section 8 - Vacancies:** When a vacancy on the board exists mid-term, the secretary must receive nominations for new members from present board members two weeks in advance of a board meeting. These nominations shall be sent out to board members with the regular board meeting announcement, to be voted upon at the next board meeting. These vacancies will be filled only to the end of the particular board member's term.

**Section 9- Resignation, termination, and absences:** Resignation from the board must be in writing and received by the Secretary. A board member shall be terminated from the board due to excess absences, more than three unexcused absences from board meetings in a year. A board member may be removed for other reasons by a three-fourths vote of the remaining directors.

**Section 10 - Special meetings:** Special meetings of the board shall be called upon the request of the President, or one-third of the board. Notices of special meetings shall be sent out by the Secretary to each board member at least two days in advance.

## ARTICLE V - COMMITTEES

**Section 1 - Committee formation**: The board may create committees as needed, such as fundraising, tournament, preservation, etc. The board chair appoints all committee chairs.

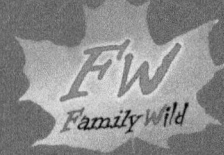
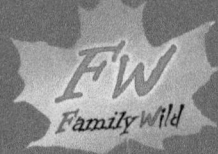

# By-Laws

**BYLAWS OF FAMILY WILD-** _____ **Chapter**

**Section 2 - Executive Committee**: Three to six officers serve as the members of the Executive Committee. Except for the power to amend the Articles of Incorporation and bylaws, the Executive Committee shall have all the powers and authority of the board of directors in the intervals between meetings of the board of directors, and subject to the direction and control of the full board. Committees assigned by the board of directors work on specific issues facing the organization. Standing committees, such as an Executive Committee or Finance Committee, should be outlined in the bylaws, whereas ad hoc committees can be created for a time period set by the board of directors.

**Section 3 - Finance Committee**: The Treasurer chairs the Finance Committee, which includes three other board members. The Finance Committee responsibilities include developing and reviewing fiscal procedures, fundraising plans, and the annual budget with staff and other board members. The board must approve the budget and all expenditures must be within budget. Any major change in the budget must be approved by the board or the Executive Committee. The fiscal year shall be the calendar year. The Finance Committee shall submit the annual reports to the board showing income, expenditures, and pending income. The financial records of the organization remain public information and the Finance committee shall make these reports available to the membership, board members, and the public.

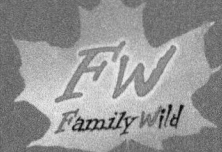 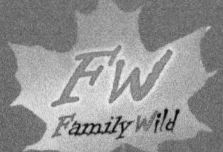

# BYLAWS OF FAMILY WILD-

_____ **Chapter**

## ARTICLE VI - AMENDMENTS

**Section 1 - Amendments**: These bylaws may be amended when necessary by two-thirds majority of the board of directors. Proposed amendments must be submitted to the Secretary to be sent out with regular board announcements.

**CERTIFICATION**: These bylaws were approved at a meeting of the board of directors by a two-thirds majority vote on _____.

(Date)

_____        _____
Secretary                                                           Date

_____        _____
President                                                           Date

_____        _____
Vice President                                                    Date

_____        _____
Treasurer                                                          Date

_____        _____
PR Director                                                       Date

_____        _____
Board Member                                                  Date

_____        _____
Board Member                                                  Board Member

# Vision Statement

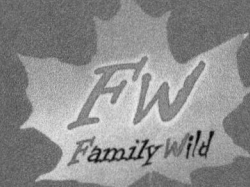

Visit us at www.familywildprogram.com

## Like us on Facebook at Family Wild

*Family Wild*

**Bringing generations together celebrating family, friendship and outdoor fun.**

# Mission Statement

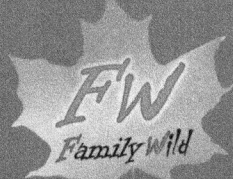

## Family Wild

**Family Wild**

*strives to pass*

*on the historic*

*North American outdoor*

*experience while creating*

*__FUN__ opportunities,*

*activities, events and forums bringing*

*generations together in family group*

*celebrations of each other and*

*the great outdoors.*

# *Family Wild*

## About the Authors

Kim Nunneley holds a master's degree in comparative religion and a certificate in holistic healthcare, both from Western Michigan University. M.W. Nunneley graduated from Central Michigan University, and is a local athletic coach and credit union employee. Both have written over 30 books. The couple lives on 50 wooded acres in northern Michigan and enjoy their cottage on the nearby lake.

Parents to Robbie & Ian, Ashley, Joshua, Courtney, grandparents to Gabriel, Izzy, Nathan & Will, Kim & M.W. deeply love their family time in nature and sharing this passion with others.

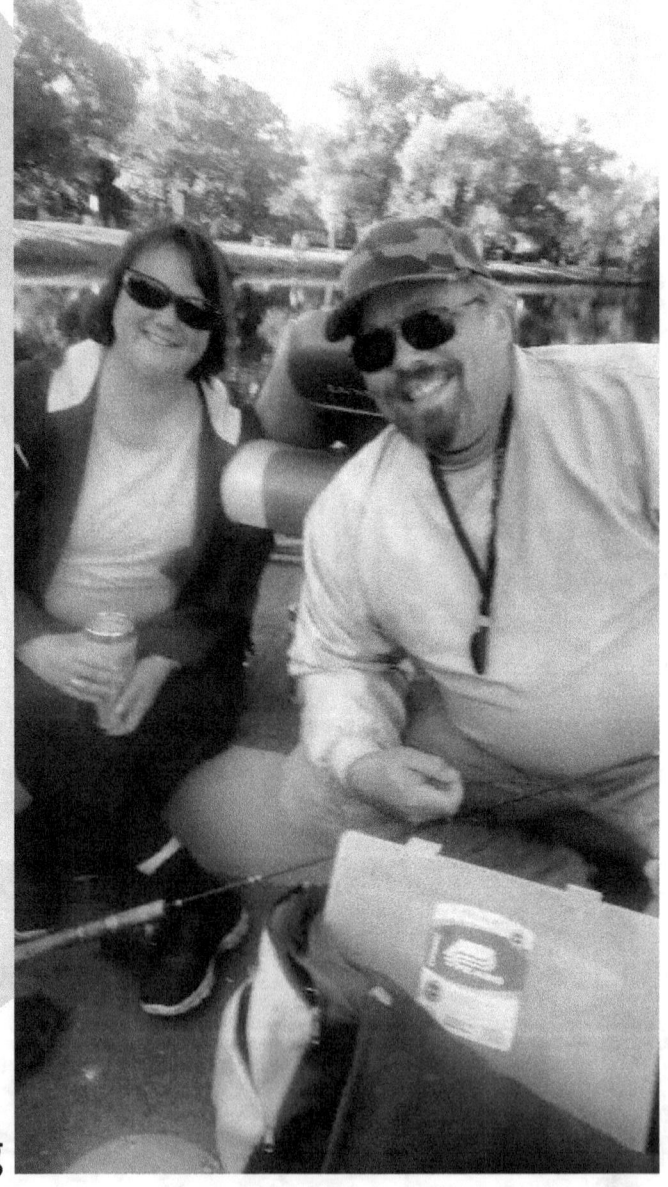

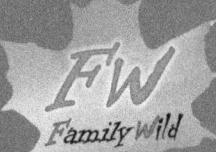
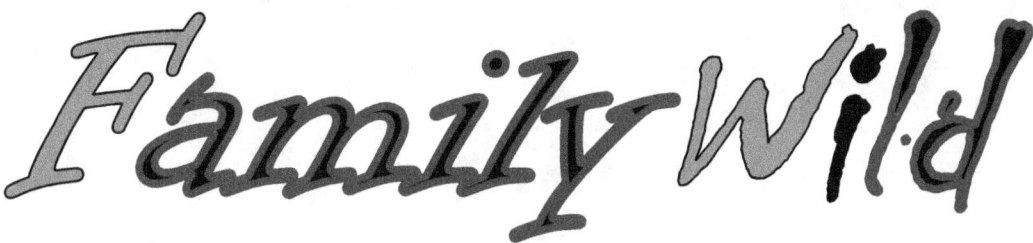
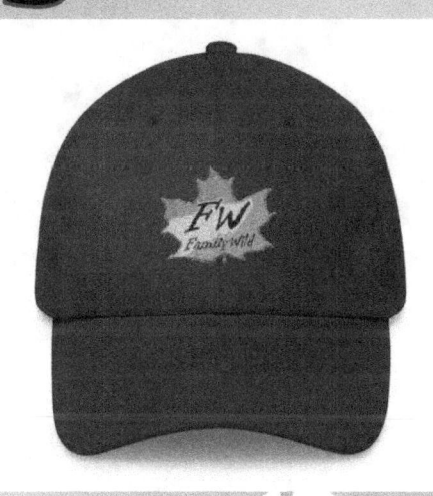

www.ingramcontent.com/pod-product-compliance
Lightning Source LLC
Chambersburg PA
CBHW081145180526
45170CB00006B/1938